Wise

As

Serpents

Godly Wisdom
for the
Christian Entrepreneur

Jack Bailey

DIAKONIA PUBLISHING
GREENSBORO, NORTH CAROLINA

Wise As Serpents
published by Diakonia Publishing
Copyright © 2008 by A.D. "Jack" Bailey
ISBN: 978-0-9800877-5-8

Cover art by Rob McGowan
Book design by Jeff Pate

For information contact:
Diakonia Publishing
P.O. Box 9512
Greensboro, NC 27429-0512
www.ephesians412.net
diakoniapublishing@hotmail.com

Or you may contact the author directly by visiting his web site:
jackbaileybusiness.com

Acknowledgements

Many authors have a stable of helpers who research information, help edit or write a lot of things that go into a book. I am sorry to say that is not the case with the writing of *Wise As Serpents*.

I want to give acknowledgement to my wonderful wife and partner, Mary, who never complained that the writing of this book was a Saturday afternoon, Sunday night or vacation project. She always encouraged me to complete this book and was the first person in my life to tell me that I was a good writer. I just never saw myself that way. I thought I was just good at expressing my views. Mary never once doubted this book would be a good story to tell. My confidence came a little later in the game.

I also want to thank Rob McGowan, who designed the book cover and Jeff Pate of Diakonia Publishing. Rob has always been an encouraging fellow believer and Jeff has been much more than a publisher. During the course of this book, both men have become my friends.

Finally, I want to thank twelve people from Word of Life Family Church who signed up for my "Life Together" group. We met once a month in our home using the manuscript as a teaching tool. When I saw their reaction, my confidence rose beyond belief because they "got" what I was trying to teach from this book. This group of twelve didn't realize it, but they became my focus group for the final touches.

Of course none of this would have worked without help from Holy Spirit, who I believe prompted me to share some of the things I learned the hard way with others in order for them to avoid the same traps.

Praise for *Wise as Serpents*

"Jack Bailey has done a masterful job of bringing to our attention the humbling, challenging and inspiring steps a Christian business leader often faces. His lifetime of experience is well worth reading for leaders in all fields."

R.C. "Dick" Hudson, President/CEO Hudson Building Supply Co., Virginia Beach, VA.

"I have known Jack Bailey for several years and I not only value his financial insight and wisdom professionally, but I have gleaned much from Jack personally. He has served on the board of directors and is currently the head of the pastoral compensation committee as well as chief financial counselor here at Word of Life Family Church. Jack possesses a wealth of business knowledge and practical sense from a biblical perspective. "Wise as a Serpent" can provide wisdom that will be the catalyst for a successful, thriving business. This book is a must read for any entrepreneur who wants to maintain a successful business venture."

Rich Fennell, Pastor, Word of Life Family Church, Burlington, NC

"This book is a powerful practical guide through the murky waters of how a Christian can successfully fulfill the Bible's command to be in the world, but not of it. Jack's clear use of Scripture, its application to business problems and their answers make this book a tool that should be offered in every church bookstore or book table. The summaries and questions at the end of each chapter make this book an ideal manual for small groups. Jack also has made the differences between ministries and business so clear that it will remove all confusion and guilt. He is highly transparent using his experiences; as well as others, to illustrate each of his principles."

Dr. Lynn Lucas, Pastor, Fountainhead Congregation, East Northport, NY, Nationwide Teacher and Convention Speaker.

Behold, I send you forth as sheep in the midst of wolves. Therefore, be wise as serpents, and harmless as doves. [Matthew 10:16]

Preface

■ I've had this book on my mind for awhile. It contains information that I believe should be shared with Christians who are entrepreneurs and who are doing their best to use Christian values in the business world. I believe there are many of us in business who are confused about using Christian values in the day to day, dog eat dog world. Thoughts swarm through our mind on how to do things God's way and still win in this environment. *What do you expect of me, God?* Ever think that?

Once I heard it said when a good businessperson becomes a Christian, they lose all common sense. I've been involved in some situations that looked as if that were true. Part of my opinion is due to some of my own silly decisions. Seldom do I meet a Christian in business who does not expect to be successful. Yet, I meet many who (a) were doing fine (according to them) *before they accepted Christ,* (b) believed it was the Lord's will they prosper *(but couldn't understand why they weren't, unless it was all the devil's fault)*, (c) or believed the more money they gave to ministries, the more profit they *would make whether they used good business judgment or not. Already we see a for-*

7

mula for disaster, right?

Having made some mistakes myself and having counseled many others through hard financial business choices, *I am of the opinion if we try to mix "religion" with common sense and general rules of business we will pay the price. Usually, it is a pretty high price at that. If we use Godly wisdom and common sense, we will win every time.* I have written this book believing that just as sure as there is Godhead (Father, Son and Holy Spirit), there is a devil. Now most Pastors and Teachers never point out several things in the Scriptures that define the difference between God, who is Love and the devil, who is evil. *Many believe Satan is a fairy tale and God is the Universe. Very few ministers seem to be able to explain how we fit into the equation.* Making matters worse, they never seem to relate (*in a business sense*) how our own choices, our desires, lusts, expectations, fears, faith, integrity, experience, education and just plain ability helps determine our outcome. It's our own fault because the Bible is clear on all those matters. *Let's face it; some businesses are dead from the beginning because of their owners. Some are dead because they begin with a bad idea and despite this fact, they still expect God to bail them out...*

On the other hand, most pastors and Bible teachers don't understand the business world. *In fact, some of the most anointed pastors I know are the worst businessmen I know.* So they depend on business people as a conduit to supply the much needed funds to fulfill the Gospel. *That's how it should be!* I believe that many ministers who begin to believe the Bible's prosperity message, if not very careful, will soon get swept up in faith decisions that have very little or absolutely no business value. Jim Baker was a prime example of a man whom I believe was called to do the Lord's work, but tried to become a developer. *I met Jim Baker once and concluded he really meant well, but when it came to building a big scale development, he was like a blind dog in a meat market.* He did not know how to build a project on paper, much less track the actual cost because he was out of his element.

A Christian making poor business decisions can hurt a lot of people while never once intending to do harm to anyone. Truly, I have never thought Jim or Tammy meant to hurt anyone, much less damage the reputation of Christianity.

Christians in business come in all shapes, sizes and background. Some come from the street, some from main line churches, some from Pentecostal or Charismatic settings some are Catholics and some are Jewish. Basically, they all agree that once they gave their heart to Christ, something changed. Most will agree that their spirit was renewed. They know their sense of right and wrong heightened, that their desire to follow after the Ten Commandments was real, but sooner or later everyone will agree that even though the Spirit of God now rests inside their spirit as a Guide, the battleground is in the mind. *God might have renewed their spirit, but they were still carrying the same baggage.* The only difference was the peace thing. They know they never had that before.

The apostle Paul understood that when he said, "Don't copy the behavior and customs of this world, but let God transfer you into a new person by changing the way you think. Then you will know what God wants you to do, and you will know how good and pleasing and perfect His will really is." (Romans 12:2 NLT)

Hey, most of us aggressive enough to be in our own business are already a little hard headed. *We are quick to ask God to move mountains; and when He takes too much time, we tend to start with our own heavy equipment. Usually, that's another formula for disaster.* If you are a Christian in business for yourself, it can become confusing, *especially if you do not spend enough time in the Word and in prayer.* I know some of you are already thinking, *"Man, I don't have time to get my work done and spend time with my family, much less spend hours in study* and prayer." OK, it's your choice, but that's not smart. You have got to figure out what you expect from God, but first you had better figure out what He expects of you.*

For example, I believe any congregation during a worship service, with everyone singing and raised hands, or kneeling with eyes closed, or whatever, singing the words "Open up the windows of Heaven, Rain down, rain down" are praying and believing God for different things.

A sick person is asking God to rain down His healing power. A broken-hearted mother could be asking God to rain down His power to change a wayward child. A disappointed young man or woman could be asking God to rain down His power to help them find a mate. The pastor is probably asking God to rain down Wisdom for him to lead his flock. A young high school or college student could be asking God to rain down the direction of their next step in life. Remember, God told Moses He was I AM! *I am what? I AM BIG ENOUGH FOR WHAT-EVER YOU NEED!*

One of the congregation could also be a sick and tired entrepreneur, who has done everything he can think of to get his business off the ropes. He has prayed, read the Word, consulted friends, talked to his pastor, his dad, his wife, and still owes a boat load of debt that is due immediately. It looks like nothing positive is happening. He knows if something good and/or supernatural doesn't happen soon, he is going to be in one of the most embarrassing messes he can dream of… I guarantee that person is asking God to rain down dollar bills and get rid of his debts. He is ready to do anything to get out of his mess. He knows it is out of control and out of his hands.

I have never met a Christian business person who wanted to hurt any creditor, who wanted to be late paying anything, or who wanted to shave edges off of his commitment to deliver his products or services. They all want to do it with honor to God and with integrity. They want to be a beacon of light in their own community. The thought crosses his mind, *"God, why are you doing this to me?"*

To add confusion to a Christian in business, he is confronted with an anointed preacher like Kenneth Copeland preaching that it is God's will to prosper us while another anointed preacher like Rick Warren is admonishing us to only serve God, and nothing else. *If you're not careful, you will get spiritual whiplash.* In fact, you could almost decide that you are wrong if you're interested in anything except serving God twenty-four seven. *The thought comes, "I probably shouldn't even be in business. God is punishing me because I didn't become a mis-sionary". Stop it, already!* You would have to be Biblical illiterate and stupid to believe you did not have to make a living and support your family. In fact, if you believe God is the one who gives us power to get wealth and Jesus said He came that we could have life more abundantly, why would you not believe you are to prosper greatly? The bottom line is, *if God placed a desire in you to be an entrepreneur, then be a good one. If He did not, you should forget the idea because it takes commitment.*

Most Christians in business believe they should do what they do better, with more success than a non-believer. They will also tell you that they believe people look to them as an example.

What they won't admit is the fact that they are bewildered and sometimes wonder if God has deserted them. Once they decide that's not the correct approach, the next thing they conclude is that the devil defeated them. *What did James say about a double minded man? He gets nothing he asks for.*

Most Christian entrepreneurs are big givers. They give to their church; they give to ministries they believe in; they give to the poor; and they even believe it is Godly to give a bigger tip to a waitress after a meal in a restaurant while telling her that God loves her and so do they. Down inside, *they are hoping that the waitress will respond, that they can lead her to the Lord, and that God will notice they are not only running a Christian business, they are working for Him. (Hey Lord, look, I'm doing your work, so how about you doing mine?)*

They base their life on what Jesus said about giving. "Give and it will be given to you. A good measure, pressed down, shaken together and running over, will be poured into your lap. For with the measure you use, it will be measured to you." (Luke 6:38 NIV) Most of us who have practiced that know it works in the long run without a doubt. *So, we are looking around, trying to find how to measure out a shovelful instead of a spoonful, so we get truckloads back. Especially in our business.*

So, what happens when you have given and given, you have followed every Biblical principle that you can think of and that every Bible teacher has preached on TV or in church, and you are about to go broke in your business? You *are embarrassed. You feel worthless as roller skates on a fish...* You do not want to give your Heavenly Father a bad name because you failed. You do not want to give your church a bad name. You do not want to face your family as a failure because you have preached God's prosperity and said you believed that it works. *You conclude suicide isn't an option because that would land you in hell.*

Most of all, you do not want to lose the faith you have built over time. What are you missing? What have you done wrong? You have heard testimonies from Christian business owners who say that after learning from their mistakes, they had more business than ever. They had more profit than ever. Why does it seem like the Word is not working in your business life?

I have written this book for you and I believe it will help you if you will read it carefully as I share some of the things I have learned. I have had a lot of victories. I have also made a lot of mistakes. *I learned much more from my mistakes than from my victories. I hope you can too.*

I hope as you read this book, you don't think for a moment I am trying to toot my own horn by using personal examples. No, that's not the case at all. Frankly, I don't know how to explain it to you any other way. Time and time again I have seen the Scriptures reveal themselves to be the truth, and whether I like it or not I have come to a sound conclusion: *God is always right whether I miss it or not.* It will be the same for you. It is my hope that several of these truths jump out at you and that you can use them to become a successful Christian in business.

If any of you think I'm a little cynical at times it's because of a lot of lessons learned the hard way. It's like an optimistic parent is one who lets his sixteen year old have the new car for a date; a pessimistic parent is one who won't; and a cynical parent is one who did. *Been there, done that.*

1 You Are Operating a Business, Not a Ministry

A double minded man is unstable in all his ways...
[James 1:8]

■ *You had better get this straight! There is a big difference between running a business and running a ministry.* Yet, they both contain so many of the same elements. Someone who ran a business when they were a hell raiser, made money and chased after the wrong things, will become confused if they fail as a Christian. Failure will also be just as confusing to the Christian who never raised hell, always made their ends meet, paid their bills on time, yet never had to rely on the market place, competition, employees and cash flow to survive, much less make a profit.

It is a known fact that most start up businesses go broke during their first three years of operation. It is also a known fact that most of those who bellied up didn't have a short term or a long term plan. They didn't know how to track either profits or cash flow. In other words, bookkeeping was something they just did not have the time, expertise, money or knowledge to do, so they were broke months before they knew it. It was just a matter of time for a deficit of cash flow to show up. *Bulletin! Most small businesses judge their profit by*

14

how much money they have in the bank today. Most big business' judge their profit by a balance sheet and P&L Statement. Either approach, if that is the your only approach can land you in big trouble.

Whatever business you own or run, if there were a way to find out whether you were making or losing money every hour and whether you were digging a hole for a cash flow deficit at the end of every day, I would say, "Go buy that system." *The trouble is, there is no such system.*

John L. McCaffrey once wrote, "The mechanics of running a business are really not very complicated when you get down to essentials. You have to make some stuff or provide some services and get somebody to pay you more than it cost you. That's about all there is to it, *except for a few million details."*

People who run their business by how much money they have in the bank on *that particular day always run in circles.* After Friday's payroll, they feel like they are broke, but by Tuesday after collecting some Receivables they feel like they are on top of the world. By Friday, the cycle starts all over again.

More sophisticated ones operate their business with appropriate cost accounting, as well as Profit and Loss statements at least monthly. They trust their Balance Sheet to tell them what ratio their Current Assets and Current Liabilities are. They look long and hard at their profitability. They have X dollars in the bank that day, They have X dollars in accounts receivables. *Man, they think, that adds up to Umpteen Thousands of Dollars.* Then they look at the accounts payables and maybe they are four times what they have in the bank today, but that's OK because they have *six times that amount in receivables.* This kind of thinking is convenient to ignore the payments that are due this week, next week and the next month for phones, rent, equipment payments, future payrolls, taxes that will become due over the next few weeks.

The owner thinks, "The Profit and Loss looks good. The Balance Sheet looks good. I am on top of the world" because that is *exactly what that pony-tailed economics professor told him to look for.* He says to himself, "God has blessed me with wisdom and a good staff, good financing, good sales, good contracts and favor! In fact, this Sunday, I am going to give $10,000 to the church building fund! *There is no way I can go wrong, right?"*

Did you know you can go flat broke while making a good profit? I made this statement to someone and he looked at me like a deer looks at headlights. Yes, you can be showing a great profit on your sales or services. There is no doubt that you have more than enough in the bank and in Accounts Receivables to pay off all your Accounts Payables.

But, what happens if you have one main customer and that one fails to pay timely or never pays? What happens if you have many customers who are tied to a particular segment of the economy and that segment is all of a sudden in the tank? Will they look after their own interests and hold their cash or will they pay you? You guess. You are last person they intend to pay. *Once they decide you need them more than they need you, there is usually a big adjustment in the business relationship. They use the golden rule! They now have the gold and they will rule what you get.*

Sometimes a study of Scriptures can be misleading without using common sense along with it. In (Proverbs 10:4 NLT) it plainly states, "Lazy people are soon poor, hard workers get rich." I believe that is *a* total truth. However, it is not *the* total truth. No one can argue that if you are going to run your own business whether a saint or sinner, you had better be ready to get up earlier, work harder and stay later than your competition. That is a matter of survival. *In most cases, it is the only way to keep a business afloat, much less grow it.*

While you are doing Proverbs 10:4, you had better be paying attention to Luke 14:28, which admonishes us, "Don't begin until you count the cost. For who would begin the construction of a building without first getting estimates and then checking to see if he has enough money to pay the bills? (TLB) *Now if that scripture ain't talking about cash flow I don't know what is. These words came out of the mouth of Jesus Himself.*

I know some of my good sisters and brothers are saying, "Where is your faith?" I could write another book about how God has honored my faith. He has pulled me through some very bad circumstances as a human being and a businessman. I know about faith and how it works. I also know that God is not going to change the law of gravity to accommodate my bad choices. He is not going to change economic laws and He is not going to run rough shod over every saint and sinner in the business world to accommodate my lack of knowledge and failure to use wisdom. He will also, I believe, allow me to make mistakes in order to learn. *Did you ever think what would happen if God kept bailing you out of every business mess you continued to get into?* You probably wouldn't learn much wisdom.

It has always irked me to no end when I have heard a big mouthed wicked successful businessman say, "Cash is king." Under my breath I would whisper, "No big mouth, Christ is King."

Over the years I have come to understand that the world's economic system is basically built by greed and fear. I know that the love of money is *the root* of all evil; and I know who the root of all evil is. I am also aware that we are to use our wealth for good causes, and I am very much aware that "the wealth of the sinner is laid up for the just" (Proverbs 13:22) and the same verse tells me that I should leave an inheritance not only to my children but to my grandchildren.

Let me give you some advice. You had better first make Christ King over everything you have before you venture off into business. Then you had *better be aware that cash is king over you paying your bills on time and you had better not forget it.* You had better ask for and receive by faith God's Wisdom to manage your profits and cash flow. You had better be careful

17

of debt.

After much study, prayer and experience, I have come to believe Rule # 1 in business.

Rule # 1 in Business. If you are going to be a giver to the Kingdom, pray that God show you how to tithe, give alms, and accumulate at least enough cash set aside in guaranteed funds to run your business for a least six months without receiving any of your receivables.

It may take you a few years to get in that position, but that should be your goal. However there are many similarities between business and ministry. Here are a few.

- **It needs people to function properly**
- **It needs a market to serve**
- **It needs good leadership**
- **It needs a plan to serve its market**
- **It will need cash to start up**
- **It will need cash to maintain its momentum**
- **It must choose good people to depend upon**
- **It must be constantly looking for new ways to serve its public**
- **It must give a service or product that people believe in and can depend upon**
- **It will generate a lot of unforeseen overhead especially during start up.**
- **It must bring in steady income if it is to survive and prosper**
- **If it fails it will give its leaders a bad name.**
- **If it does not pay its bills, it will close down.**

Take a look at the big differences between a business and a ministry on the next page.

BUSINESS	MINISTRY
It should hire people who are skilled at what the business needs regardless of their belief system	It must only hire committed Christians who are committed to the ministry and to the Lord.
It should pay well, and readily fire anyone who does not perform. Any employer must have a well known reward and punish system.	It must operate by faith and must work with employees who are committed but need time to learn.
It should look at its competition and figure out ways to outsmart them, gain their share of the marketplace and scratch to stay in front.	It must give to its brother and sisters in the same area and become known as a giver to anyone who needs help, even if it is a rival.
It must look at the end of every day and decide what it could have done better to lower cost or to up its unit price of whatever it produces or sells.	It must look at the end of every day and decide if it really helped someone and if it is doing the will of God.
If an employee is found to be on drugs or alcohol the judgment must be made as to whether he is valuable enough to the business for you to try, at least once to rehabilitate him. If he doesn't contribute to the business, let the ministry worry with him. He is a liability.	If a staff member slips into drugs or alcohol, the judgment must be made to pray with him, counsel him, and to bring him back from the depths of his bondage. That is your mission. Surely, you cannot turn out your own.

19

There are many other differences, but you get the gist of what a vast area of differences there is between running a successful business and a successful ministry.

I first began to realize that in 1988 when I was an elder at Rock Church International in Virginia Beach. At the same time, I was President of the Chesapeake Chapter of the Full Gospel Businessmen's Association. Somehow, it seemed that both Rock Church and CBN would direct people who were in financial trouble to me for counsel. *At first, I was honored, but after a while it became a challenge.*

I loved that period of my life spiritually. I was among about seventy five elders in Rock Church in Virginia Beach, headed by Bishop John Giminez and his wonderful wife Anne, who is the church's pastor. Today, they have over four hundred churches established around the world. It was a spiritual high to work with such anointed people. When John started the "Washington For Jesus" campaign in 1988, I was privileged to be one of a four member "Green Team" who had to pray through how to finance and plan an operation that could get one million people on the Capital Grounds on time. That took a bunch of faith since only 85,000 could get in by bus or train and plane on a daily basis.

At the same time, my business was doing very well. I had a Cessna 421 and could fly Bishop John and myself around where he needed to go within close range. A highlight of my life was having my pilot fly Bishop John and I to Northern Virginia for him to preach to Joe Gibbs and the Redskins team that went to the Super Bowl that year. I got to meet many of them. I was especially happy to meet Joe Gibbs and his wife. *The first thing I noticed about Joe Gibbs was he had every hair in place. I sat directly behind him during the service and could not take my eyes of how perfect a head of hair that man was blessed with.* It could have been because I was losing my own hair. He too, wrote a book about learning how to be a Christian businessman based on his experiences as a race team owner and a coach. He has been a real role model. *Now, to get back on track with my point!*

I was also very privileged to meet Pat Robertson, a man whom I had greatly admired, not only as a teacher and politician, but as a businessman. He was truly an example of a God-lead businessman with a ministry. Yet, he was very practical. Truly, he used Godly wisdom and discretion daily. *For the life of me, I cannot understand Christians who despise Pat. I can see how the secular journalist don't believe a word he says. They don't have a clue about faith, healing, prosperity, peace and it all sounds like a ruse to them. Well, big deal, the Bible said that is how it will be in the end times.*

First, I noticed that a lot of people would go to work at CBN because "the Lord sent them to Pat Robertson." That would especially be true when Pat started some new big venture that helped fuel the cost of building Regent University that now sits on those wonderful grounds. I would find myself sitting across a desk listening to some forlorn looking Christian telling me how *Pat Robertson was vicious or uncaring. My next question usually led to their being fired by Pat or his subordinates.* When I began to probe, many times I would find they were not a tither. Then, I would have to tell them all the reasons that God couldn't bless what they were doing, because if you believed Luke 6:38 about giving, you had to believe Malachi 3: 8-9, that said if you didn't tithe, you were robbing God and cursed with a curse. The ones who learned from the experience immediately began to tithe and get on track. *The others would just not show up anymore.* That suited me just fine because I was tired of messing with them.

Those early years taught me that people have some really crazy, mixed up ideas of who God is and what He expects. It seemed like they saw finances as something spiritual or mystical. The question kept coming back to me. *"How did this guy get into financial trouble to begin with?"* Most of their problems had to do with their attitude toward profits in business or just how to pay their bills and have any money left over. *No kidding, it was like some of them thought it was God's will for them to be poor, or to have some bad luck, or whatever.* Then one day it hit me. *They didn't look to God as their source; they were looking to Pat Robertson as their source.*

I remember counseling a former employee of CBN who could not believe that Pat Robertson had shut down the whole division where he worked. Even though that division failed, he couldn't understand why CBN did not find something else for him to do. Look, it is very Biblical for an employer to dismiss an employee if that employee is not needed to do the work. In fact, the words servants and masters used in the Bible is many times the same as employer and employee.

For example, words used for servants in the Old Testament, written in the Hebrew language are "abad" a primitive root word which means "to work," by implication "to serve." The Aramaic word "gibbar" is also used to describe a servant as "valiant' or a "warrior." I believe any employer would want employees who will work, serve and will be valiant warriors at their assigned tasks. That is the Biblical version of servant. *Now, weigh that against the attitude that everybody has a right to a job.*

On the other hand, the word masters especially in the New Testament comes from the Greek word "kurios" which means one "supreme in authority" or "controller." Let's face it—the Biblical version of a master is basically a boss. I am sure human nature hasn't changed. The boss who gained respect from his employees could get more work done in a shorter time period 2,000 years ago as well as today. The employee who does not perform for his boss will be fired or demoted today just as well as then. Nothing has changed, except... *A ridiculous philosophy taught in high school, college and the media, that is the employer is a hostile, self-absorbed crook and the worker is a victim who is at his mercy.* No, the facts are, the employer couldn't have a business without the worker, but *equally true is the fact that the worker wouldn't be able to pay his bills or grow financially without income from a job furnished by the employer. In my humble opinion, everyone in this country should be glad we have entrepreneurs who provide jobs, cash flow into communities and pay taxes.*

Now about this "everyone has a right to a job." *What a crock.* Jobs are created by a business making a profit and needing people to work for that business' welfare. If the business ceases to make money, the employee is not needed and neither is the boss. *It is in everybody's interest to keep most businesses going as long as they can make a profit.*

Unions, for example, are useless as they seek to gain big benefits for a moment only to bring their employer to its knees. Then the employer shuts down plants. lays off workers and no one makes a profit. The union bosses are the only ones still wearing $500 suits. *Yeah, I know, you are asking, Jack are you politically incorrect enough to publicly say you are against unions. Are you claiming that unions are against Biblical principals?* Yes, I absolutely am saying that. As a young man, each time I got even got close to a union organization, I saw their upside down thinking. When I became a Christian, I knew I was right about it all the time and the reasons why. In fact, if a child of mine became a union official, I would be ashamed. *Unions were necessary 100 years ago, but today, they have outlived their usefulness. In fact, they are a detriment to society.* Any worker in the United States of America who cannot find work to provide for his family just isn't looking very hard. *If a Christian is wholly looking to his union to provide for him, he has his trust in the wrong place.* Most unions are corrupt from the top down.

I counseled so many Christians who had no concept that the reason they were hired was to generate enough *profit to pay for themselves, their superiors, and their portion of the company overhead and still generate a profit.* How could you expect to stay employed if that isn't done? No one teaches this simple concept in today's high schools or colleges, much to the detriment of young people who start out in life thinking that somebody owes them a job. *The apostle Paul was right. If you don't work, you shouldn't eat, unless you are unable (II Thessalonians 3:10). Then Christians should look after your welfare, not the government.*

TRANSFORMATION VS. CONFRONTATION:

Even though every ministry has to confront things and every business must transform things, a very basic difference between a ministry and business is this:

A ministry is based on transformation. It works to transform the lives of those it touches; it transforms entire neighborhoods, regions and even nations. It transforms by espousing love, determination and true concern for human welfare. One of its primary purposes is transforming the soul (which is the mind, will and emotions) of individuals and families. That takes a mindset of caring, discernment, of bending over backwards to help even when it isn't asked for. It requires believing in individuals, in the power of God helping transform the spirit and soul. A ministry must surround itself with people who believe like its founders or those in charge. It must be diligent to see that no staff member embarrasses the ministry by lewd or bad behavior. It must be careful to give to other ministries and be completely non-critical, even though they may not agree. It must show love, joy, peace, patience, gentleness, goodness, meekness, faith and temperance.

A business is based on confrontation. It must first confront its competitors and work diligently to gain more share of the market place. (*or that competitors business.*) It must work night and day to build a better service or product than its competitor. It must confront its employees with the challenge of outperforming its competitors. Without wanting to, a surviving business person will soon understand that many of his employees who draw paychecks are not at all dedicated to anything except quitting time and a weekly check. Therefore, the manager must confront his employees. Though the business owner may be a devout Christian and adopt those ethics, *he will soon learn that he had rather employ a heathen who will do his job without goading than a Christian who stands around the shop or water cooler and won't work.* A business owner soon learns that the banker *who adores him while things look rosy is the very banker that he can't please when things get tough. These scenarios always produce uncomfortable confrontations.* Furthermore, he learns that almost everything the company is involved in is based on litigation and he has to have a good lawyer. Then he learns that he must constantly confront his lawyer (who has 100 other clients just like him) just for his time. (While the lawyer finds time to always bill him.) He has to confront his lawyer and press him to confront other parties who are trying to take anything they can get from his business. There are always confrontations to collect money that is justly due. There are always confrontations with competitors, employees, people looking for a free ride, and also with suppliers that are always overcharging for their materials and services.

Having said this, *Can you imagine any business owner who decides he is going to run his business like a ministry? That is like an ice hockey player deciding to make his living as a lady hairdresser!*

I can speak directly to that, because I made the mistake of thinking my business was my ministry and that I was the *priest* of it. If you look hard enough, you can find all kinds of scripture to fit that mindset. *I found out the hard way I was supposed to be the CEO instead of priest. I should have made the money by being better at what I did and give it to the priest (my pastor or ministry per God's directions.)*

I learned that I should care for my employees as long as they performed. I never hated my competitors, but worked to be better. I learned to love all my employees like God does us, but also to never stop holding them accountable for their actions (like God does us.) I also learned that Psalm 112 was right on target. It reveals the perfect businessman:

v1. Praise ye the Lord. Blessed is the man who fears the Lord, who delights greatly in his commandments.

This sets the tone for what a Christian businessperson must be from the inside out. He must praise the Lord for all he has. He must fear Him with reverence, and must delight greatly in what His word says.

v2. His seed shall be might upon earth: the generation of the upright shall be blessed.

The Christian businessperson must believe that if they conform to His ten commandments and receive His grace, not only they, but their children will be blessed. Every parent wants their children to be blessed. Notice, the businessperson's own generation should expect to be blessed.

v3 Wealth and riches shall be in his house; and his righteousness endures forever.

Every Christian in business should get up every morning thanking God for whatever wealth and riches he has and he should remember his right standing with God through Jesus Christ. Remember the Scripture: "He made Him who knew no sin to be sin for us that we might become the righteousness of God in Him." (2 Cor. 5:21 NKJV) This means that even though our feelings, actions, or words may not agree, but because of Jesus' sacrifice, we are the righteousness of God because He did it for us. That is what is so beautiful about grace.

Don't stop there. Grace is wonderful, but so is His wisdom to get wealth and riches in your house.

Sidebar Thought: My mother, who is in heaven had this saying, regardless how many hours I would work or how much I accomplished, even though I was church going, heavy giving and all the other good things, she would say, "Well, money isn't everything, you know." She was right, but her inference was (and her life proved it) that you were supposed to be satisfied with just enough to get along. You shouldn't have all those big ambitions and think about making fortunes. *I don't see that anywhere in the Bible!* I resented that thought then and I resent it now. My answer usually was, "Yes mom, I know. I have been poor and I've been rich. I like rich better."

v4 Unto the upright there arises light in the darkness.

The next few words show why light always comes through for this person. Look at it.

he is gracious and full of compassion and righteous. v5. A good man shows favor and lends, he will guide his affairs with discretion.

The Hebrew word for favor is "katabraheuo". It means beguile of reward, frequently denotes opposition or intensity. The Hebrew word used for lends or lendeth, is "paraineo" and it means to admonish, exhort, recommend or advise. Surprisingly, the word used for discretion is "suntuche" which means an accident or chance together.

My understanding of this verse is that this businessperson, because he is gracious and full of compassion will show favor and even lend money to someone (expecting to be repaid) who even though he does not entirely agree with them. He will exhort them and advise them, hoping that it all works out. *The bottom line is, if your gut tells you, err on the side of being a liberal giver rather than a taker.* I have done that many times with employees. Sometimes I got burned, but most of the time, I built loyalty.

Barnes Biblical Notes basically puts it like this. "A good man shows favor to help his fellow man achieve happiness here and in the world to come. He lends and joins the bond between lender and creditor expecting to be repaid. Guiding his affairs means that he will uphold and furnish a living by managing his business and that the word discretion shows his judgment. The notes go on to say, "A man who neglects his 'affairs', who pays no attention to his business, who is indifferent whether he is a success or fails, is a man who gives 'just so evidence that he is a stranger to true religion.'"

v6. Surely, he will not be moved forever; the righteous shall be in everlasting remembrance.

The successful businessperson is fixed, stable, able to weather storms, is not easily moved by adversity, has faith, has grit, will persevere. Everyone, friend and foe alike will see that. *Faith and persistence is a big factor in whatever you're doing.*

v7. He shall not be afraid of evil tidings: his heart is fixed, trusting in the Lord.

Trust is key. The successful businessperson knows that whatever happens to the marketplace to interest rates, if he keeps his trust in the Lord, things will work to his favor. *Remember faith and persistence. Whatever you do, ask God to show you the next step. Then move by faith.*

v9. His heart is established, he shall not be afraid, until he sees his desires upon his enemies.

The successful businessperson recognizes his enemies are those who are trying to destroy him and his business for personal reasons, for both natural reasons and spiritual reasons. Don't forget, if you are a successful business person and a big giver, *you will gain some attention from the dark side.* I have never met a successful Christian business person who did not recognize this truth. When the enemy attacks, keep trusting God, use good sound judgment, don't get sidetracked and you will win. *Every time and usually over time.*

v10. He has dispersed, he has given to the poor, his righteousness endures forever, his horn shall be exalted with honor.

The Hebrew word for dispersed is "pazar" and it means to scatter whether enmity or bounty. That's pretty clear. If you have been giving, don't quit just because you are in a down period. When things are going well, don't forget to tithe and give to the poor. You will build your legacy by implementing these principles. But, don't be foolish. Don't ever give for a show, because sooner or later you will be giving away some creditor's money that doesn't belong to you.

POINTS TO REMEMBER IN THIS CHAPTER:

- Operate your business as a business. It is not a ministry.
- Expect greatness out of yourself and your employees.
- Don't hesitate to fire someone who is costing you profits or who will not be a team member.
- There is no such thing as a *right* to a job. You are not required to keep anyone who is not profitable.
- Put your trust in God. Use Biblical Principles. It is the only way a Christian business person can continue in today's environment.
- Never give up. If you have to bring something to a close, move on to the next phase.
- Respect and love ministries. Give to them as you can with God's help.
- Guide your affairs with good sense and discretion.

WHAT IS CHAPTER ONE ALL ABOUT?

1. Why do you think most small businesses fail within the first three years after start-up?
   · They don't have a _____plan
   · They don't know how to _____.

2. Your goal should be to have enough cash to operate your business without receiving any of your accounts receivable for at least _____months.

3. A ministry must hire committed Christians who are committed to the Lord and the ministry. A business should hire people who _____.

4. A Christian employee should know that he should generate enough profit to pay for themselves, their superiors,

_____.

5. If a ministry is based on transformation, a business is based on _____.

6. A business owner or manager must confront competitors, employees, his banker and his _____.

7. Name at least three promises you see in the life of the businessperson shown in Psalms 112.

   · _____
   · _____
   · _____

8. Why do you think light always arises in the darkness to a Psalms 112 believer?

- He is gracious and _____
- He shows favor and _____
- He guide his affairs with _____

9. Why is a Psalms 112 believer never afraid of evil tidings, no matter how severe?

- His heart is _____ trusting in _____.
- He has _____, he has given to _____.
- His righteousness _____.
- God will exalt him with _____.

2 Trust God, Yourself & Your Spouse (if applicable)

If God cannot trust his own messengers (for even angels make mistakes), how much less men made of dust. (Job 4:20 TLB)

■ I was fortunate to have grown up in a home where lying, cheating and stealing were not allowed, period. My parents both practiced what they preached. From an early age, I was taught that "a man's word is his bond and how you act when no one is looking is what counts." I grew up with a profound sense that honesty was always the best policy. I had *heard* of people who would lie or cheat to better enhance their position, but I thought they were in a giant minority. At one low point in my life, I thought that explained why my parents were not very successful financially. In fact, to them if someone in the community sued someone else over almost anything, *they looked upon him as a failure and a crook.* They believed strongly that you should be up front with what you were thinking, and in their eyes, if you showed a sign of greed you were a "hog." I grew up believing you could make a better success in life with honesty than you could with deceit and guile. After all these years, I know that's true, but we have to recognize the world for what it is.

I have to admit that most of my business setbacks have

occurred because *I somehow thought people I dealt with could be trusted to treat me like I wanted to treat them.* My wife Mary tried to point that out to me several years ago, and after four or five slaps across the face, millions of dollars lost and having to pick myself off the preverbal ground, I began to wake up.

My first experience at such a thing was when I was President of Bailey & Associates. We were a very successful road building and site development firm in Northern Virginia. I had been pretty fortunate to build such a company by my mid thirties. One of the people who helped me build that company so quickly from scratch was a man I will call "Seth."

I was all of thirty-six years old and Seth was about fourteen years older. He was smart, well traveled, educated and a wonderful employee. I decided to reward him, so I started a separate Land Company, giving him one third of the ownership. The construction company continued to grow and it was low bidder on several Virginia Department of Highway projects around Alexandria. At the same time, we were low bidder on the Route 17 by-pass in Fredericksburg, Virginia. It was all we could do, with the management we had, to just "keep up the pace." *I am finally reaching my dreams, I thought.*

At the same time, I had started a concrete plant with other partners and a development project with a local attorney. You might say, I had spread myself a little thin, but I was confident in not only myself, but in the ability of Seth and those around me. I could see within a few years, I would reach the multi millionaire status I so desperately craved back then. My bible was *Think and Grow Rich* by Napoleon Hill. He laid out the twelve principles of success and I was bound and determined to follow every one of them. One of the things Hill espoused in his book was to "surround yourself with a like-minded group." That is easier said than done. If you don't believe it, make a study of David who fought so hard to remain King of Israel only to have his most trusted priest and his own son betray him. Yet, it is evident, they told him what they wanted him to hear for a long time. Be careful of your "roundtable." *President Reagan was right. Trust-but verify.*

Seth and I were trusted confidants, or so I thought. He was in charge of operations and had some good men working under him and I was the "rain maker" and business manager. The sky was the limit. I trusted Seth like I thought he trusted me.

What I didn't account for, was Seth and his wife in North Carolina had become estranged. I just did not catch it when she and their daughters would come to Northern Virginia to visit once in awhile. At other times, Seth would spend his weekends in North Carolina. I thought their relationship was a little strange, but his family wasn't my focus at the time.

Without telling me anything, Seth and his wife decided to split. I noticed he worked more weekends, but so did I. I did not realize that he had met a beautiful twenty eight year old airline stewardess and they were *madly in love or badly in heat at the time.* Over a period of several months, it became more difficult to reach Seth via the radio. In those days before cell phones, the best way for us to communicate was by two way radio.

I noticed he was particularity hard to find early in the mornings. On top of that, the overpass project we were building as a "fly-over" on Duke Street in Alexandria was losing money. I was shocked to see that it had lost over $200,000 in about four months. The more I talked to Seth, the more he assured me he was giving his undivided attention to the Duke Street job. What I did not know was, his girlfriend had a high rise apartment near the Duke Street project, *so he was giving his undivided attention to things in Alexandria alright, but it wasn't the construction project.*

Not only that, but the Route 17 project virtually had little or no supervision and the daily reports showed us moving a lot of excavation, but no one was careful to see the cut and fill slopes were on grade. Finally, after riding through the Route 17 project and taking stock, I began to ask questions.

I didn't realize what a profound effect Seth's behavior had on all our men in operations. They felt abandoned. *They wondered why in the world I hadn't already done something before things got in such bad shape. I felt like a full-fledged fool.* Seth, my best friend and confident advisor must have decided that since I gave him ownership in land we owned and gave him unlimited power over operations, he didn't have to worry about what I thought or the company's profitability again. *Because I rewarded him above what he had earned, he didn't feel obligated to "let it all hang out."* In fact, like most people do, he decided he didn't have to work as hard since he now had ownership. *Here's a bulletin! If you own all or part of any business, you had better understand longer hours and harder work come with the deal! If you don't want to go that route, then get a job putting hubcaps on pickup trucks in a Ford assembly line and complain about your union.* At least you have regular hours and know what you can earn.

I fired my best friend Seth in the middle of a road on a big project in Caroline County, Virginia with tears in my eyes. It took me years to work out of that mess. When Seth left town, he was immediately hired to take over a land development operation in Tennessee. Frankly, I was glad he landed on his feet, that was until he took the best young superintendent I had with him. To his credit, he married his Piedmont Airlines lady, but I made a big mistake trusting him for too long a time without verifying his performance. I made the mistake of trusting him like I could be trusted.

Finally, after selling out my interest in the road building company to a Washington firm, I entered into the development business in Fredericksburg, Virginia. It was a wild time for me. I have said that I changed occupations, wives, oil in my car and friends in 1973. It was also when I met and married my long time best buddy, Mary. She had such an impact on me. She loved me, she loved my children and she was a worker. On top of that she was smart and beautiful.

Before we were married, I told her that she had might as well understand that business would always come first. Of course, I did that because my previous marriage had been a nightmare, at least to me. My previous wife never thought I was cultured enough, never calm enough, I never stayed at home enough, and I wasn't a pipe smoking, rocking chair rocker or country club goer enough. The fact that I worked seven days a week surely didn't help. Frankly, I look back and realize that rather than stay at home and argue, *I would just start another business. It was easier to fight debits and credits than a woman whom I thought needed special attention.* That probably wasn't a fair opinion, but that is how I saw things back then. I was just as wrong as she was. Neither of us was fulfilling our roles as parents (Biblically speaking) though we belonged to a church. I respect her very much as the mother of four of my seven children and wish her the best in life. I would never intentionally do or say anything to hurt her. Enough said.

After Mary and I married, I could not believe how wonderful and understanding she was. I kept thinking, "I know before this year is over, I am going to find out she is not *really* this nice and understanding." So, I piled it on. I told her that even if we were headed on vacation and the business needed me, I would turn around and go back to the business. She just smiled and said, "OK."

As our first anniversary approached, I began to feel downright ashamed. So, on the night of our anniversary, when I told her at the office we would go out for dinner, she replied, "No, let's have a quiet dinner at home. I'll cook us a steak dinner." That just added to the guilt, so I had my speech all prepared for that night.

As we sat together in candlelight with the children upstairs, I began to confess to her. "Honey, you know when I told you that business would always come before you and the children, I really didn't mean it. You know that I love you and you come first in my life."

I was expecting a shocked reply or at least one of astonishment. She looked into my eyes with that blond head slightly cocked to the right and said, "Oh, I have known that all along. I just wondered how long it would take you to figure it out." *Man, I thought, "This woman knows more about me than I do."* That has been very true, and besides that, I found out early on I could trust her with anything, anywhere.

So, here we were. We created Ole Forge Townhouses, just 46 miles south of Washington, D.C. We had developed the land, built and sold thirty-two townhouse units in the first phase and as we began the second phase of sixty-nine units, I realized I had better hook up with a builder I could trust. I did or so I thought. He had worked for the civil engineer who owned a share in the development. I was surprised to learn he was a bonafide builder. I worked out a contract with him to build the first phase. That phase sold out so fast, when we came to the second phase, I thought in order to give him an incentive, I would give him one third interest in the development company. *Wouldn't you think I had learned my lesson with Seth?* He and I had built a close relationship over the first year and as we entered the second year, I thought it was a little unfair for me to push him so hard to build as fast as we sold without allowing him to share in the profits. (Now that is how I would have liked to be treated if I were in his place.) *That was a mistake.*

The corporate structure of ownership in the Urban Development Corporation was an engineer, an attorney, and myself. During the first year, I bought out the others and owned it outright. I thought I would treat the builder who I will call

"Travis" like I would like to be treated. He was a good family man. He had children and I felt close to him and his wife. Mary did not feel quite so close and I should have followed her lead. *Another bulletin! Women have a better radar system than we men do. They seem to hear the Holy Spirit clearer than we do.* Wish I had figured that out years ago.

Mary was in charge of sales and she sold out the second phase of sixty-nine units before we finished the first sixteen under construction. All we needed to do was get them built, inspected and closed. We were already grading the streets and laying water and sewer outfalls for the next phase of one hundred nineteen units.

Oh by the way, I forgot to tell you that the local member of the Virginia House of Representatives came to me and said he was not going to run for another term and he asked me to take his place. If I'd had one lick of sense, I would have thanked him and said, "You must be nuts." Instead, I began to ponder over his request. "How about this," I thought. "Here I am, a transplanted North Carolinian who is divorced, remarried and yet respected enough to run for a state office." That was unsound thinking and had nothing to do with running the business.

So, I took Mary and two of the younger children, Angie and Joe in our RV to Virginia Beach to make a decision about running for public office. It rained all weekend so we were bound inside the RV. The kids drove me wild in that small space. I'll never know whether I made the decision in guilt *(after all I had been told by the political leaders that it was time for me to put back into the society that had been so good to me)*, or *maybe it was ego.* In any event, I decided to go for it. *Important lesson! Never get involved deeply into politics or anything else that will take up your time until your business is so well established, it can operate without you.*

Six of us ran for two seats. Of course one of the incumbents would go back in. That put five of us vying for the other seat. It was an experience. It caused me to take my eyes off the business and trust my son Jack to look after the development even though he was still in high school and Travis to look after the building.

To make a long story short, I wound up third in the election, which was a respectful showing, but the four of us who were conservatives spilt the vote so badly, the second seat went to a liberal, Boston-reared professor at Mary Washington College. The only consolation I had later was he was voted by the Richmond *Times Dispatch* as the legislator with the least influence two years in a row.

Suddenly, I woke up and realized that Travis was behind on his building schedule in Olde Forge development. He had screwed up the pouring of the covered swimming pool we built as an amenity, and his building program for the third phase was not keeping up with sales. *That was so unlike him. He had been such a trooper. Surely, this could not be a repeat of my earlier stupid mistake with Seth, I thought.*

One day Travis did not show up for work. I couldn't find him. When I investigated his whereabouts, I learned he had purchased an RV, left his wife and had run off with another woman. I could not believe it. *Again, I gave him over and above what he had earned and now I was the idiot that would pay for it.* I used to wonder if I had some kind of sick way of getting acceptance or did I honestly want to treat people like I wanted to be treated. Frankly, looking back years later, I can honestly say I learned a lot from it. First, I learned that I did it because I had always hoped someone would "give" me a big break in business and I would surely show them how I would excel. Secondly, I learned that it is absolutely stupid to give someone a share in any business or venture unless they earned it over and over. Otherwise, they took it as a gift and it absolutely did not motivate them to multiply their efforts. Human nature is exactly what the Bible says it is. Selfish, self centered, and without morals or integrity.

One thing for sure. I had never been a builder, but now I was one. Not only were one hundred and nineteen units going up in phases, but we were about two-thirds complete with building a shopping center of which I had pre-leased about 80% of the space. *Suddenly, I felt like a one-eyed cat watching ten rat holes. There weren't enough hours in the days to cover the bases.*

Then a few days later, as I was clearing land for a sand and gravel pit on a farm I owned jointly with a local doctor, I received a phone call. It was from my attorney and close confidant Gordon Gay. He said, "Jack, you had better get over to my office. There is a guy here who claims he owns your development company. He has shades, a black shirt and a white tie and the two goons with him look even worse."

By this time, I was totally ready for a fight with about anyone at any time. Gordon was right. I will call the guy with shades "Kurt." He not only told me that he had controlling interest in my development company, but he would bring me down. He said that Travis had sold him his stock (*the stock I gave him*). "I am such an idiot," I thought. I knew that Travis had only one-third interest in my company, regardless of what this clown said. He said he had been told that I had been taking out monies from the development company to the detriment of Travis. I knew that wasn't true.

My answer to him cannot be printed in a Christian book, *but I basically told him he was a minority stockholder in a closed corporation and that was like a spayed dog at a breeding clinic. He might be here but he couldn't do anything.* He left and said he would get back in touch.

I desperately needed help from a builder. Kurt was a builder and developer from Richmond and after a few days, he called and very nicely asked if we could meet. I said sure, but he had to leave his goons at home. He came, but brought a guy I will call "Rob" who worked for him and was a builder who had built houses and commercial buildings around Martinsville, Virginia. Rob said he had gone broke and Kurt had bailed him out. We met at a local restaurant and Kurt made his pitch. He said, "You know, Bailey, you have been much nicer to me than I would have been to you if you tried to do this to me in Richmond. I have come to realize that I only bought one-third of your development company, but I also realize that you need help in finishing what you have started. If you mess around until interest rates rise to get those houses built and you don't get your tenants into that shopping center you are going to be in more trouble than you are in now." We both knew he was right.

He said, "To protect both our interests, how about letting Rob finish all your building construction?" I was more than skeptical. I told him I would think about it. So, I began an investigation of Kurt through my suppliers and others. His credit was sterling. I heard how he was a little ruthless, and how he had bought out or closed down some businesses. Yet, on the other hand, I found people who thought he was a genius. Some said that he always made money and was very good in legal matters. In fact, the more I heard about him, the more I sort of liked him.

After a few days I called him back and told him that before we went any further, I wanted to look at Travis' books. Kurt claimed he had them, and in order to avoid any liens or lawsuits, I wanted to see if Travis had been paying his bills as I paid him. To prove I had not been taking money from the company (as Travis had accused), I told Kurt he could see my development company books. We would do it by renting two rooms in a local motel with an open door between the two of us. I would have my books in one room and he would have Travis' books in the other. We both would have our independent accountants go over the others books and settle this thing about my integrity and honesty.

The day came and as we allowed our accountants to go over each others set of books, Kurt said, "C'mon Bailey, let's go downtown for a cup of coffee and talk." I opened the door to his red Cadillac knowing I had better be careful. We drove to the Mary Washington Inn and sat outside. I glanced at a sign that said Winston Churchill had stayed there during World War II. *"You know"* I thought, *"I kind of like this guy's brass."*

I was in my early forties and Kurt was in his late fifties. There we sat—two businessmen, both confident and proud that one could outsmart the other. As we talked, he agreed to release Rob from his company and let him enter into a separate contract with me to finish the shopping center and Phase III of the development. It seemed reasonable to me. *I was desperate for a builder. I should have listened to Mary. She said something was "just wrong" with Kurt and Rob.*

Ironically, Travis had paid his bills, and Kurt could find no wrong in my books, so we departed and later I drew up a contract with Rob to finish the building I so desperately needed. I thought, "Well, this should work for Kurt and I." After all, Kurt would profit from the development company's gains.

Rob seemed like a very personable and likeable guy. His wife Elsie was even better. She would come to Fredericksburg and spend time with him, and one night Rob and Elsie invited Mary and I out to the Sheraton Inn for dinner. The setting of the inn was gorgeous. The owner had spent millions converting an old barn to a first class restaurant and had built a superb motel.

Mary, Elsie, Rob and I finished dinner and the two of them began to make a pitch for us to sell out to Kurt. Both Mary and I were reluctant to go any further. When we got home, we both said it was as if we were in some kind of evil revival with the two of them saying, "Won't you come?"

From that day forward, I never trusted Rob and had every right to do so. It was too late though. What I did not know, but found out in court discovery later that he and Kurt had a written contract that Kurt would share in one-third of whatever Rob profited while on my project. It was obvious what happened. *I should have seen it coming. Kurt was going to try and do what he had set out to do and that was take over my development. He wasn't satisfied with one third, he wanted it all.*

I noticed that Rob would not finish units we had sold, but would work on units started but not sold. He was doing everything to place us in a cash bind. I began to place all communication in writing, knowing it would wind up in court. The longer it took, the more interest I paid to keep the project going, and the fewer units we could timely close, the cash flow became tighter. Then interest rates rose and it was a matter of time.

One Friday afternoon Kurt showed up at my office in his red Cadillac, red jacket, dark blue shirt, white tie, and dark glasses. I noticed he began to drink every day at about four o'clock. Rob was always at his side, doing everything from pouring his drinks to lighting his cigarettes.

He sat down across from my desk and proceeded to tell me what a helluva mess I was in. He knew almost to the dollar what I owed. It was obvious Rob was Kurt's informer. He said to me, "Bailey, I have a way out for you. All you have to do is not pay any more bills on this project. In fact, I suggest you pocket everything you can over the next four or five months, that should be several hundred thousand, and then let the creditors file liens. The title company will have to come in and pay up. You'll get money, Rob will get paid and eventually the creditors will get paid by the title company."

I knew that meant all I would have to do was bankrupt the company and find a way to pocket the money. *There was no way I was going to do that! I wasn't a born again Christian, but my upbringing would not allow me to even think about it.*

I told him he could flat go to hell. He jumped up and shouted, "I will see you broke." I reached across the desk and pushed him in the chest and said, "*You are not man enough.*"

Well, the war was on. While we were fighting, a recession set in. My lender, Cameron-Brown with headquarters in Raleigh, NC became more broke than I was. They couldn't fund the project's completion even though there was plenty of equity and I was in the middle of a lawsuit with Kurt that would have made perfume smell like a skunk.

I had a land company that sold a parcel I purchased when it was a big gully and had filled in with basement excavation I had cut out from Phase IV of Olde Forge. I had it sold to a service station company for $300,000. The sale closed and as my attorney took the documents to Stafford County Courthouse, Kurt's attorney beat him by about fourteen minutes. He had filed a *lis penden.* I soon learned it was Latin for "notice of suit" and I could not get my money. In fact, it took five years to get my money.

The next thing I knew, Kurt's attorney filed a suit against Mary and I, claiming we had dissipated assets in order to not pay creditors. Two years later I found out his only claim was that I had used the asset of dirt from Urban Development to fill the gully by Stafford Land Corp. It saved money for Urban rather than truck it for miles. Because it profited Stafford Land, he claimed it was stealing. Needless to say, I won that one hands down. He filed the "case in chief" under a false claim that I owed Kurt (who had bought out Rob) for construction work. The suit he filed was for $153,000.

Five years later, after both of us spending fortunes, I finally defeated Kurt in the Virginia Court of Appeals. In the meantime, we had generated 5,967 pages of testimony. Kurt's attorney, the title company's attorney and mine (even though

Gordon allowed me to do the leg work and charged only a pit-
tance compared to the others) charged over $1,000,000. All of
this over a $153,000 suit. Guess what? When Kurt lost, he sued
his attorney and won back about $300,000. *The only good thing
came out of it all was, I gained a world of legal knowledge, but it
would have been cheaper and easier to have gone to law school.*

**Rule # 2 in Business: Never trust anyone who can gain dollars
by seeing you lose, no matter how reasonable they sound. And
never give anyone ownership in anything you own unless they
pay a fair price for it. They never appreciate a gift that costs
them nothing.**

The previous story doesn't end there. On July 4, 1974, on
the way back from a disastrous meeting with Cameron-Brown
the day before, Mary and I fell to our knees and asked Jesus to
come into our hearts, to forgive us of anything we had done
and guide us. We both committed our lives to Him that day.
That was the day we really became born-again Christians. As a
token of notice, I received a box about three weeks later from
Mr. Harrison, the owner of an apartment complex in
Fredericksburg, which was named Hosanna Heights. My son
Jack and others had used my heavy equipment to grade his
site and I had visited him several times. In that box was a
Living Bible. Inside the cover were written these words. "To
Jack Bailey in appreciation of your meritorious performance
at Hosanna Heights." *He had dated it July 4, 1974.* It was as
if God had personally sent me a note, saying, "*I saw you re-
ceive My Son. You are now mine.*"

"Wow," I thought. "God had Mr. Harrison write that on
the same morning I accepted Christ." My life has never been
the same.

Two weeks later, one of our tenants set fire to the shopping center to collect insurance. I noticed though, I had a

strange peace that I had not known before. I had gone to church much of my life, had even taught Sunday School, but I guess I had not quite made the cut until July 4th, 1974.

God has a way of turning bad into good. Years later, I received a call from Kurt, who had bought all the remaining land of Olde Forge from Cameron-Brown after foreclosure. (*Kurt had the money to ride out the recession*) His call was about a $150,000 sewer tap deal I had made with Stafford County on Phase IV of the subdivision years earlier. I had installed an off site sewer line and a pump station in return for several pre-paid sewer taps. In the meantime, the sewer taps had increased in price and the county had "lost" any records of my having pre-paid them. Even though I had moved to Virginia Beach, and was busy in building and developing, I agreed to meet Kurt and help him. Frankly, I respected his intellect and his grit. We had been in a costly fight, but I knew I had beaten one of the most astute businessmen and legally minded men as well as the most ruthless I had ever come up against. *Somehow though, my outlook changed a little and I looked forward to seeing my old enemy. Over those months, I had forgiven Kurt and had been praying for his salvation.*

When we met in a hotel in Fredericksburg, he laid out his problem with the county and I told him how and where we could go to "remind" them of the deal. I testified in court the next day and Kurt got his sewer taps.

Later, I heard Kurt had brain cancer and had only a few months to live. I began to realize that I had stood in my living room in Virginia Beach many years earlier and forgave Kurt before God as an act of my own will. God had honored that and when I heard that Kurt had brain cancer, I was livid. You cannot pray for salvation that long for someone and idly sit by while Satan kills them with cancer. *The seculars and unbelievers just don't understand that once God's love enters you through Christ, you love people that you use to hate. It is the world's most*

*powerful force. Although in anger I had told Kurt to "go to hell"
before I was born again, the Holy Spirit had prompted me to pray
him out of it!*

I called and told him I would meet him in his office in Richmond. He looked bad; he had lost weight and was still smoking. I began to witness to him, to tell him how Christ had changed me from the inside out. All of a sudden I heard myself say," Kurt, have you ever accepted Jesus as your Savior?" He said he thought he had when he as a kid. I said, "No you haven't. Do you want to settle this thing once and for all?" He said yes, so I led him in the sinner's prayer. He told me the doctors had given him only three months to live. I felt a strong urge to lay hands on his head and I did, shouting out, "I curse the root of this cancer and command it to die in Jesus' name. Father, I thank you for your healing power to heal Kurt." Then, I found myself speaking in other tongues.

His office workers in the next room began to make noise like they thought I had gone off my rocker. I gave Kurt my phone numbers and told him I would be back in touch. As I walked out of his office, I could feel the stares of his staff and his son, who all knew we had been great enemies. *It was a long walk across the parking lot at his office.* I couldn't blame them for wondering if I was doing something to get even with Kurt.

Kurt and I talked a lot over the next few months. I knew he had a mistress and that she bore him a son, yet I knew he would not leave his wife at this stage. His mistress was considerably younger and somehow he gave her my phone number. I will call her Renee. She became a Christian and the next thing I know she and Kurt asked me to meet them at the Sheraton Hotel in Richmond at a Norvel Hayes Healing Service. *At least he was coming to the right meetings.* On top of that, he was staying sober.

Sitting in the lobby after the service held by Norvel, Renee began to tell me how I should talk to Kurt. She said she wanted me to tell him that he could not have two wives. I listened and thought to myself "How did I ever get into this mess?" As I asked Kurt what he thought, he said he didn't understand why he couldn't have at least two, because he had been reading about Solomon and he had about nine hundred wives. *At least he had been reading the Bible. He was as serious as he could be.* Talk about asking God for wisdom, I did many times in counseling with Kurt. The desperation he felt between his two families, the fact that he knew if he died he would go to heaven finally caused him to get tired of the whole scene.

About five days after the Norvel Hayes meeting, Kurt called to tell me he had beaten the cancer. He then told me something over the phone that gave me goose bumps. He said, "Bailey, that day in my office when you laid your hands on my head, I felt something warm begin at the top of my head and go through my body. I know God healed me that day." I need to make a point here. He had led such a life away from the church; he just couldn't understand the importance of hearing and hearing the Word. I told him, "You know, Kurt, God didn't heal you just so you can sit around and continue living. If you don't get the Word inside your spirit, you won't have the faith to continue beating the one who is trying to kill you."

During that time a catastrophe happened to Rob. He still lived near Martinsville and worked for Kurt in Richmond and in Northern Virginia. One late Sunday night, he had stopped at a McDonald's in Ashland, Virginia for a cup of coffee. He probably was trying to stay awake long enough to get to his rented quarters in Stafford County and be on site first thing Monday morning. The police investigation revealed that a drug gang mistook Rob and his fancy pickup truck to be that of a drug dealer who had stolen from them. Rob's body was found in the parking lot of an apartment complex in Richmond.

As the days wore on, Kurt's desire to look after his new family became utmost in his thinking. He was caught between a very jealous older wife who felt like she had put up with him all these years and she was not about to accept anyone else sharing his fortune. I am sure Kurt's older son was very much vocal in the matter, because he had known all along about the affair. My guess is, when push came to shove and the son and the wife decided they might have to split up a $20,000,000 fortune, things got hairy.

Kurt asked me to come and see him. He told me that he had a sizeable first mortgage he was holding on a property in Northern Virginia and that he was assigning it to Renee. He also told me that he had a sizeable Certificate of Deposit he had made out to her for their young child's education. He asked me to take him back for a treatment at the hospital because his brain cancer had reoccurred.

I knew that day that it would not be long. Here was a man who had truly reaped what he had sown. He was forgiven and he knew it. He was ready to go and leave this mess he had created behind. He did, within a month after my visit. He had beaten his doctor's predictions by over a year. If I have ever seen a situation that was proof positive that making money is not the total answer to being a businessman, this was it. It settled in my heart forever that if we made all the money in the world and didn't serve God, love and cherish and support our family, our church and our community, it was all in vain.

The story should end there, but it didn't. After Kurt's death, when Renee tried to get the mortgage assigned to her and stored in his Richmond office, Kurt's wife and son sued her and did their best to void all that Kurt had tried to do for her. I was called to be a witness. I figured Renee had the case won when the opposing attorney began by asking me about my relationship with the Kurt. When I told them about his conversion, his healing and his desires to look after his "other" family, it didn't last long. Renee won her case.

On the way back from Richmond to Virginia Beach the

evening of the final trial involving Kurt, I could not help but think out loud, *"Kurt, you old rascal, you were a pain to me from the beginning and now after your body is in the ground I am still having to go to court because of you. Yet, I will be glad to see you in heaven."* Bringing that man to the Lord is one of the most rewarding things I have ever done. I am looking forward to talking to him when I get to heaven.

Though I made a mistake in trusting Seth, Rob and Kurt, God finally turned it around for good. Only he can do that.

As you read this chapter you can find plenty of things that I did wrong. I was too sure of my own ability to overcome anybody and anything. That caused me a lot of pain. I became distracted too easily and thought I could handle more at one time than I really could.

Out of it all I got a good legal education. In fact, it caused me to buy two sets of law books and when it comes to commercial and real estate law, I believe I have seen it in action. Law makes a lot of sense to me, because most of the time it is practical. Kurt gave me an education in street fighting law that I will always relish. *He taught me pressure points to apply to any opponent in business and get his attention.*

My dad was exactly right in his country boy wisdom when he told me more than once. "You can never tell what a man is made of until there is a dollar involved." I have also observed that different people, including Christians, have a different view of what honesty is. That is why a good dose of understanding in Proverbs and James (those are what I call the two business books in the Bible) will help anyone get their business thinking straight. *Wish I had known all that earlier.*

I am very fortunate that Mary is my best business confidant. She will be honest with me and I can tell her anything, good or bad. That is very important and I know that if things do not work out as planned I will never hear about it later. She has truly known as the apostle Paul wrote, "how to be abased and how to abound." She has come from rags to riches more than once and has never complained.

However, I have known a lot of people who cannot confide in their spouse. *If that is your case, go tell somebody else you trust that has no dog in your hunt*. I am serious about the title to this second chapter. Trust God, yourself and your spouse, only if applicable.

Be careful who you trust in business. It will take you too long to overcome the mistakes.

CONCLUSIONS:

- Trust no one but yourself, God and maybe one other person in business. As for your immediate staff, like President Reagan said, "Trust but verify."
- Stay focused on what you are trying to accomplish.
- Never, never give someone something for nothing in business. It will bite you.
- Do not overload yourself with more than you can handle.
- Do not trust anyone who has something to gain if you fail.
- Never stop working until you get out of your mess. Perseverance again!
- Trust God to help you always see the "next step."
- All things finally work together for good, if you don't quit.
- Study the Word of God for direction and do what the Holy Spirit says to you. (He can't direct you by the Word if you don't place it inside of you first.)

WHAT IS CHAPTER TWO ALL ABOUT?

1. Do you have a tendency to believe that most people are honest? Yes   No

2. If you are an Owner or Manager and you trust your next subordinate so much you do not question what he/she is doing, what effect will that have on the "front line workers." They will feel _____.

3. What can be the effect if you always treat your subordinates the "way you wish someone had treated you." They will_____.

4. If you are building your business and it is not financed well enough or staffed with long time subordinates and you are asked to become deeply involved in local or political, time consuming things, you should

_____.

5. If an adversary in a business deal suddenly begins to "play nice" and change his direction should you (1) be on guard (2) accept what he says or (3) look for what angle he is playing.

6. Though you eventually become friends with adversaries like Jack and Mary did with Rob and Elsie, should you trust them at face value? Yes_____No_____

7. What should take place between you and anyone who wants to own a part of your business? They must

_____ for it.

8. If your adversary becomes a born again believer, do you change your attitude toward him? Yes_____ No _____. Is it still wise to trust but_____?

9. What do you think happens to your attitude after you have prayed for years for an adversary's salvation and you hear he/she is at the point of death? You feel like

_____.

10. When you are overloaded with circumstances, whether you brought it upon yourself or not, what is the first thing to remember? Trust God to help you always

_____.

3   Partnerships Seldom Work Long Term

Now, I beseech you brethren, by the name of our Lord Jesus Christ, that ye all speak the same thing and that there be no divisions among you, but that ye be perfectly joined together in the same mind and in the same judgment. [I Corinthians 1:10 KJV]

Christians are big on getting into business with other partners. I have had partners, been sole owner, been a minority and majority shareholder and have made it a point to find the perfect partnership. However, I have never found it. We all know about being "unequally yoked." I know some of you reading this are already thinking about some wonderful partnerships you are aware of.

Some partnerships look wonderful for awhile. Inevitably, it is a natural course for the "rainmaker" or the marketing and sales portion of a partnership to decide over time he is the most important part of the equation. That partner will decide that he is making the sacrifices. He is taking his weekends to entertain and spending his nights away from home. His political contacts are made and relationships are kept even when he is so tired he can't see straight. It is so easy for him to decide that he/she is what really keeps the company afloat. After all, he thinks, "If I didn't bring in the business we wouldn't have a business."

Steeped in operations, having to watch his costs, being

kept in the shadows, and never written about in the press, his partner soon gets tired of the game. He takes a look at his partner who seems to always be on a golf trip with a client, attending a function, flying first class, or driving somewhere to have a meal with a client, is the one who has it easy. No matter how much business his partner can bring into the front door, it wouldn't amount to anything if he (who is in charge of operations) didn't work like a dog to produce results. He is the *real* reason the business is a success.

For example, I think of two companies I observed from a distance. I personally knew the four partners involved in both companies. To outsiders, they seemed like perfect examples of working partnerships, but I knew better.

One of the companies was a civil engineering firm. I will call the firm "Hannity & Franks." I had known one of the family members for many years and had witnessed what happened from a fairly clear and neutral viewpoint. I had seen hard feelings on both sides for many years, only to be reconciled upon the death of both partners.

They were the perfect partnership. Hannity was the rainmaker. Not only was he friend to governors, and senators, but he also seemed to be connected to everyone who was "anyone" locally. He seemed to be a Democrat when he needed to be and a Republican when it was necessary. He became a member of the Highway Commission. He was so well respected; he had a four-lane by-pass named after him. He was likeable, approachable and not only owned half of the engineering partnership, but had formed other partnerships with attorneys, judges, businessmen, and CPAs to buy land within and around the city in which he lived. He was the man with whom I cut a deal to purchase 464 acres that later became a project called Las Gaviotas. He drummed up more business than the engineering firm could handle.

He was so well respected when he opened his front door in the mornings and began a short jog, other young businessmen would wait until he "hit the street" just to spend a few minutes with him. I personally knew some of them. He was idolized by many, feared by a few, and was an icon in his own hometown.

His death at fifty-two was a shock to his family and his city. His flock talked about his death for months. Some of the young businessmen who followed after his advice thought they no longer had a "connection" they could go to.

His partner Franks had been the worker in the background for a long time. He too was well respected, and was a very accomplished civil engineer. He was the guy who had slaved day and night to crank out plans and specifications for cities throughout the state, for owners and developers in the whole Tidewater area. He and his son had worked diligently in the shadows to make the firm one of the most sought after civil engineering firms in the eastern portion of the state. He was in charge of all field surveying as well as the design of city water and sewer improvements, of site plans and subdivisions.

Franks had built such a stellar reputation with the planning commissions, engineering staffs, and with mayors and elected officials of most of the surrounding cities that it was pretty much understood that if "Hannity & Franks recommended something, it would be approved."

Not only did he work a sizeable staff of engineers, but he also worked Hannity's son, who was an accomplished surveyor. There was a natural competition between the two sons. Hannity's son had prodigal son tendencies while Frank's son, an engineer himself, seemed to be more like the "older responsible son" in the Biblical story.

Like many private partnerships, the insurance policy to buy out one of the partners in case of death wasn't increased as the worth of the business increased. So, as soon as Hannity was buried, the process began for Franks to buy out the Hannity interest for the value of the insurance policy and to get rid of Hannity's son who thought he would inherit half of the firm. It was obvious the Franks family wanted the Hannity family out of the business. They were tired of doing all the work while the other family received all the recognition—at least that's how the Franks family saw things.

Observation: The partnership worked in the short term, but did not serve the intent of both partners in the end. It had long term consequences that seemed harsh and unfair to one partner's family. *Both families thought they got a raw deal in the end.*

The other example was pretty much the same situation. It was a highway, heavy, dredging and clearing firm. It was well respected from Maryland to Mississippi. One partner was the administrator and front man. His partner was in charge of operations. They were very successful and had a business generating revenue over $22,000,000 annually back in the '80s.

Both of them were in a dilemma as to what to do with their company as they approached their sixties. I met with the two of them more than once as they both decided they did not feel comfortable turning the business over to their sons, both of whom worked in the business. The front man became very depressed and finally committed suicide. The operations man immediately took over, paid off the surviving members of his partner's family and fired the son of the former front man.

Once again, it worked until something happened to one of its originators.

I have noticed many times in smaller partnerships, Christians will get with other Christians and start an operation that is not able to pay salaries to all of them in its start up phase.

So, naturally one of them goes at it full time. *It is usually the person who came up with the idea for the business that begins to devote full time to it.* Pretty soon, if it grows, it needs more capital and they all begin to sign notes at the bank for business loans. When things get tight, *(and sooner or later they will)* the non performing partners realize they are now on bank notes with joint and several obligations and they begin to question what the operating partner is doing. So many times, instead of them all working together to get through the mess, they turn on each other and start pointing fingers. The rest, they say, is history. Nine times out of ten, the partnership goes down in flames and people are angry with each other.

Rule # 3 in Business: Partnerships, whether individual, corporate or limited are only good for the time a business is in its start-up stage. The problem always comes when the business becomes very successful or when one of the partners dies, or when things become stressful. Remember, always (1) define the original ownership conditions, (2) constantly upgrade insurance policies and re-write the agreement as conditions change and (3) always have the partnership agreement clear as to how to dissolve it under any of these circumstances. Bottom line, when going into a partnership, know what the conditions are for getting out of it.

I have had my children and sons-in-law as partners, as well as people from other professions, businessmen and friends. All of them begin with hope. Most of them end with someone being disappointed. *The best model for a business is one you control. You can reward your employees in many ways, but giving up part of your control is not the best way.*

One of my most challenging partnerships began after a phone call from my old friend, Gordon Gay. I had just weathered the interest rate debacle that drove construction loan rates from 8% to 22%. Beachfront houses that I had pre-sold prior to construction could not close because all permanent mortgages were at a standstill. It was a hairy time for builders/developers and in late 1980 the rates began to subside.

Gordon Gay, my dear attorney friend said he had a man whom I should meet. The man had recently moved to Fredericksburg from California, and had purchased a large estate home in one of the most prestigious sections of that area. He had experienced a heart attack, was in his late sixties and was looking for someone knowledgeable in developing and building. Gordon thought I fit the bill and I suspect he thought I could use a financial giant to make a strong comeback as the market revived.

The man's name was Davison Obenauer. We agreed to meet him and his wife Yvonne in Hampton, Virginia after I told him that was where one of my projects was located.

He was a tall, dark haired man who looked every bit of 68, and his wife was a very pretty Spanish lady who was several years his junior. They both were well educated and personable. We met, we talked and we both promised to get back in touch at a certain time.

Frankly, I could get no "feel" for this guy. I liked his wife, but there was something about him I just could not put my finger on. Mary told me that Yvonne was alright, but I had better watch my association with Davison. She said, "You both are very aggressive and will clash."

So, since I was now a Christian, *I began to pray and ask God to tell me what to do. I didn't get a "yes" and certainly I didn't get a "no." What was God waiting on?*

Davison began to press me for a decision. I began to look at my situation and wanted God to hurry and make up His mind. I will never forget my words as I pulled out onto I-64 headed north to Fredericksburg. "Lord, I have asked you and you haven't answered. If you don't tell me something before I get to this meeting, I am going to take his offer." The world did not shake, God did not move on His throne and I got nothing. *What I should have done is turn around, go home and tell the Lord that I wasn't going to do anything until I heard from Him. Instead, I went into business with Davison.*

The first year was remarkable. Seldom does a company begin in the building/development business show a profit until after one or two years. Because we developed some of the previous properties I had controlled and the market was healing and growing, we showed a profit of $227,000 the first twelve months. *Gee, I thought, "This must be my answer."*

Davison was ecstatic and I will have to say he was the biggest dreamer I had ever met. He was also one of the biggest spenders I had ever met. Soon, because he loved airplanes, we had our own twin engine Cessna plane and were looking for deals to develop from Virginia to Florida.

We built out waterfront projects in Hampton, Virginia and frankly it was fun to be turned loose to use my imagination and energy. We contracted for 464 acres in Chesapeake and I hired an eccentric land designer and architect that was one of the best I have ever seen. He would stay up for two or three days and nights and come up with a remarkable layout, then he would crash for three of four days. He designed that flat land beside Cedar Road and colored a beautiful overview showing 763 lots, an 18 hole golf course, a country club, lakes, canals, and a lifetime care center in the middle with shopping centers up front.

I knew that Chesapeake, Virginia had never seen such a thing, so flying back from Florida, I designed a story board and a slide show that eventually won over the Planning Commission and gained approval by the City Council for rezoning that farmland to what is now Las Gaviotas.

We used the same slide show to pre-sell six million dollars in lots to builders from the first phase prior to pushing down

61

the first tree. Builders bought lots as fast as we could sell them. Mary also began to market single family lots in certain areas around the lakes and golf course that sold for figures foreign to that part of the world at that time. Times were good. The next few years saw a community rise up before our very eyes. *Boy, being a Christian businessman was cool.*

In the meantime Yvonne became very sick. She was diagnosed with cancer. Mary and I introduced her to the Lord and began to witness that God would heal her. She began to listen to healing tapes and when they learned that Kenneth Copeland was having a healing service in Tulsa at the Oral Roberts University, Davison insisted that we accompany the two of them. They were prayed for and several months later, he confessed to me that where she had lesions inside her pelvis x-rays now showed scars.

They asked us to accompany them to Mexico where they had been married. Yvonne's parents were killed when she was young, but she had been raised at a Mexican estate called Vista Hermosa. It had over eight acres of family housing under roof. It had its own chapel, its own pits for cockfights, and its own kitchens that turned out to be restaurants. Yvonne's cousins came and we heard the story of how her grandfather, who was one of the few billionaires in Mexico, had to flee through a tunnel that reached from Vista Hermosa to the backside of the adjoining mountain when the Mexican government took over his place. In fact, the Mexican government still owned it while we were there.

We still have a VCR film of their renewing their wedding vows in that wonderful chapel. It was some weekend.

It seemed that the more we accomplished, the more Davison wanted to spend money. He bought a jet and he and Yvonne would travel back and forth to California. Of course, he would charge the expenses for his trips to the company we owned. It was a hard thing to handle. I knew his financial acumen had been a driving force in our success, but I began to see things that didn't look exactly right. I was doing the work and he was enjoying his old age. I told myself that was OK. I would just work harder and make more money.

Yvonne seemed to be in constant fear that the cancer would return. No matter how much Mary and I would tell her to hold on to her faith, her Catholic guilt-ridden personality just could not seem to find rest. Then, I found that Davison had borrowed over one million dollars from her cousins in Mexico and had promised to pay it back. Whoa! *Could that be where he got all his money? Could that be the seed money Gordon Gay and I saw? Could that be the reason I got no answer from God to go into business with him in the first place?*

Yvonne grew worse and they moved her to a clinic in Florida. They sold their Fredericksburg estate home, rented a sizeable house in Chesapeake, and a condo in Florida to be near her doctors. Mary and I flew there to visit her. She was in terrible shape. When she saw us, she immediately tried to tell us something about Davison paying her cousins. He came into the room and she stopped talking.

It was evident we should part ways. I formed a company to own the millions of dollars of heavy equipment we used to develop the roads, utilities, lakes and golf course with. I sold my interest in the original company to Davison, and my company contracted with his company to finish the development. I also contracted to purchase most of the frontage of the land from Davison to build a shopping center, and to develop the land designed for a lifetime care center. We had already hired a person to head up that operation from scratch.

Yvonne died and was buried in Florida. Davison and his youngest son Leandro parted ways and Leandro showed up on our doorstep, so we took him in like one of our own. Davison claimed he had contracted prostrate cancer and flew to California for an operation and treatment. I heard later that he

63

had a penal transplant and that seemed plausible because he moved to Mexico with his young blond co-pilot.

I continued to operate the finishing and closing of Las Gaviotas. The only problem was when I bought the properties from Davison's company, he was supposed to pay off the encumbrance and put the balance into paying me for performing the development work. He drew down bank draws to pay me plus buy out my interest at closings. Instead he absconded with the money. I finally traced about $1.6 million that was missing.

The bottom line was, I was stuck with First American Bank for the balance on a $6,000,000 acquisition and development loan. Much to my surprise when I met with the bankers they were quick to tell me that they had loaned the money to the partnership because of me, not Davison. *Now that came as a shock*. I realized if I had the patience, I could have done all this without help. They could never trace where he had gotten his money either. I also had several other projects going on plus I owned an office building directly across from City Hall. Things still looked fairly good.

That is, until the great real estate depression of 1989-90 hit. I had exhausted my cash cleaning up the Las Gaviotas mess and had no reserve. It was a fiasco that took me six long years to overcome.

I was advised by my attorneys to take bankruptcy, but I refused. Today, I am not so sure that was the wise choice, but I plugged through, paid the banks or settled in friendly foreclosures, kept my credit intact and finally, after all those years was flat broke.

Of all seven of our children, thank God six of them were out making a living for themselves and that left Mary and our youngest, Ashley to plod ahead. It was an expensive lesson and you would think I would have known better. Here is what I learned.

CONCLUSIONS:

- When the Scriptures say "wait on the Lord," they aren't joking. You had better wait and get an answer even if you don't like it. *He does know best!*
- When you form a partnership or joint venture, be sure of who it is with and what each of you is to contribute. Have clear definitions as to what happens if one of the partners wants out.
- You are much better off, if you need money, to get it from investors who have a definite return for their risk, but you are totally in charge. Don't be fuzzy about that.
- Do not acquire a partner if you don't have to have one.
- More partnerships fail than the ones that are successful.
- If you are in a working partnership, work at it like a marriage. Don't forget when you trust, also verify. Verify your partner's dreams, hopes and future goals. If they conflict with yours, you have a problem.

WHAT IS CHAPTER THREE ALL ABOUT?

1. Why do most partnerships fail? The administrator, marketer or "rainmaker" believes he is the real reason for the partnership success because _____ the business would_____. The operations partner knows if he didn't work like a dog

_____.

2. Why do you think that is the case for both partners?

_____

_____.

3. If most partnerships work well during the start up stage, what usually happens when?
   · The business becomes a success.

   _____

   · When business runs into a tight spot

   _____

   · When one partner is out of the business

   _____

4. What are three things to always do when forming a partnership?
   · Define the

   _____

   · Constantly upgrade the insurance and re-write the

   _____

   _____

   · Have the agreement clear on how to

   _____

   · Bottom line is when going into a partnership know

   _____

5. The best business is one you

_____.

6. If you are considering a partnership and you ask God to reveal if it is a correct one, what should you do when you have waited a few days and haven't heard from Him?_____

_____.

7. If you are in a working partnership, work it like a

_____.

8. If you can get money for your business from investors with a fixed rate of return are you better off than having a partner? Yes_____No_____

4 We All Have a Management Style What is Yours?

For three things the earth is perturbed, Yes for four it cannot bear up; For a servant when he reigns, A fool when he is filled with food, A hateful woman when she is married, And a maidservant who succeeds her mistress. [Proverbs 30.23 NKJV]

I know the Scripture quoted above sounds a little strange, but think about it. If a servant suddenly reigns, he will have a definite management style. He is likely to manage the way he used to be managed. Take a fool filled with food and he probably thinks you don't need management and the place will run by itself. Now take a hateful woman (or man) who becomes boss and you have a nasty situation. I can think of only one thing worse, and that is a maidservant who was abused, used and berated by her mistress, and one day the mistress is out of there. Suddenly, the maidservant is in charge. I would not want to be on the receiving end of that management style.

What is your management style? *You had better understand yourself. Are you the fool full of food, or a hateful woman to those around you? Or are you like someone who has succeeded above those who helped you get to the top?*

I had always thought that my strength was managing people. All my life I had somehow been able to rally people around a cause. I worked hard, gave more than I took, and saw the benefits time and time again. I tried to set examples by asking no one to do anything that I wouldn't do myself. If someone could work eight hours, I could work sixteen. I would prevail, *or so I thought.*

It was as if I was living in a surreal world. I could not understand it. I had always looked after my employees, did my best to practice all the traits of leadership I could, but I had lost my business and my wealth by age 57. I thought, "How can this happen to an honest, hard working, Christian businessman?"

I learned a couple of things after I went broke. One, most people who have known you for years just do not believe you haven't piled up several hundred thousand dollars for yourself; and two, people have their own problems and are not interested in yours. *That's true with your neighbors, your friends and your church.* I noticed after I was broke I could go out to breakfast with some business friends and they *still allowed me to pay for it!* I soon came to realize they didn't have a clue that I was in the financial shape I had just told them about. In fact, they didn't believe it, either.

I was so disturbed that I asked Bishop John if I could be prophesied over at the church's next Presbytery. God had a sense of humor and made me sit through several services before I was called out. The prophecy was pretty clear that I was to take an advisory roll in helping others and that Mary and I would be pillars in the church. I thought, *"That's nice but what about my next business step?"* Then one of the prophets turned around and came back to tell me that I had business acumen and that I was to show a lot of young people "where I came from in life."

Since I had been praying for an answer to whether I should form a consulting business or ask someone for a job, I took that to mean I should be a consultant. Having owned or managed large organizations over the years, I have never felt as lonely in trying to be a one man show. I had gotten most of my children and some of my employees out safely and in business for themselves. The truth was, in all the selling, settling and looking out for others, I eventually cut off all cash flow to Mary and I. That was stupid then and it still is. I considered it an act of faith, since I had no other explanation.

The hardest thing to accept was the fact that I had no business. *I loved business. I missed business.* What if I never ran another business? I missed the strategy sessions, the decision making, and the adrenaline rush of sizing up a deal and finally closing it. Frankly, I thought I was going to die, but I never could find the right words to say, "I quit." I have learned over the years that I can't quit because I could never live with myself if I did. No matter what, if I die at ninety-five making a deal, *if it is honest and I would be proud to stand before my Heavenly Father and let Him see it, I will die happy.*

So, how does a guy who has been well-known both by businessmen, banks, newspapers, politicians and friends market himself as a consultant when they all know he is flat broke? If he is so smart, why is he broke? *That question haunted me. I knew I could make money for others. What was wrong with my management style?*

I looked for words of encouragement and soon found them. My banker began to tell me that he had never seen anyone stick with a mess like I had and solve it. He had helped. Of course, I knew that God had His hand in it. In fact, my banker began to recommend me to others who had real estate problems. An attorney in Newport News representing a bank in an unfinished building needed advice. I worked with him four hours and showed him how to solve his problem. I sent him a bill for $400.00 and he paid it. Wow, I thought, I am now a consultant.

I hated that word consultant. When I said it, I conjured up a vision of a used car salesman. I thought of all the "Engineer Consultants" I had listened to only to insult them because they didn't know what they were talking about. *Now I was one! Talk about eroding any pride I had left, this was it.*

I also figured out early on that being a one man show meant that the time I spent trying to market myself cost money and earned nothing. That first year was miserable. I think I generated about $22,000 in revenue. But, I had the prophecy. I didn't know how to quit and I had no where else to go. That is called motivation. The fact that I was 58 years old meant nothing to me. I had made up my mind that I was going to rebound if it "hair-lipped a skunk" and I was 85 when it happened. Besides that, I really believed it was God's will that I prosper and be in health as my soul prospered (3 John 1:2).

Then came my first big break came. A friend of mine, Bob Dagenhart contracted Lyme Disease. He was very successful as a Fire Sprinkler Contractor and a sizeable real estate owner. He and his brother had a corporation in Charlotte, NC that was losing money and had a big debt load. This was my first corporate turn-a-round job. In the meantime, I had become a Certified Consultant by the Academy of Professional Consultants and Advisors. I took their test and after consultation with their staff, I was certified in four areas. The areas were Business Turnarounds, Business Negotiations, Marketing, and Government Apportionment. I'm not sure I knew what all that meant and neither did they. *So I decided going forward was better than sitting still.*

I had sold my company car and we were down to one vehicle between Mary and I. That's how close things were. Our net worth had fell from about six million dollars to about six dollars. We still had our faith in God, each other and good health. By that time, I was sixty years old.

Bob suggested that I drive his three year old Lincoln as the official Dagenhart Sprinkler car. I drove from Chesapeake to Charlotte and rented a room at a new Hotel 8, within a block of their spacious office and warehouse. I had no idea

71

who worked there, how bad things were or what to expect. All I knew was the former Vice President of the Charlotte branch was in his late seventies and that he had Alzheimer's disease. Bob thought he had a $150,000 Certificate of Deposit in his company safe and couldn't figure out why he and his brother were constantly having to put money in the company. Later we found the old VP had used it to borrow against and had forgotten it. It had been redeemed by the bank and the money had been spent.

When the Charlotte office opened that first morning I was there bright and early to meet all the supervisors and workmen. I told them my mission was to clean up and turn around the company. I immediately received their support. Within my first hour there, I had phone calls from one of the supervisors saying they had their trucks at a gas station, but had been cut off for non-payment. I met the station manager and used my own credit card to fill everyone up and promised to get him his back debt paid.

That's how the first entire week went. I learned that the former manager lived about forty five minutes south of Charlotte and could not understand why Bob had asked him to retire. It was a challenge to go to his home and get the information I needed to understand some of the decisions he had made. I also learned that their accounts payable looked like a load and it took a week to get any kind of reading on the receivables. *Every time I thought about quitting, I would think, "This is better than the mess I just came through."*

I met two nice young men and right away we hit it off. Glenn Ravan was very knowledgeable and was in charge of several projects. Ken Neff was also bright and smart even though he was a little skeptical at first. After working seven days straight, we had a fairly clear picture of what they owed and what they had in probable receivables. The problem was, we didn't know what it would cost to finish their projects which ranged from schools in South Carolina, to the Spartanburg General Hospital to several projects in North Carolina. I worked furiously the second week so I could show Bob where he stood when he flew into Charlotte on Monday.

When he arrived he was so sick he asked me to drive him to Bank of America's branch near his office. He walked in with me, introduced me, and told them to put my name on all their accounts and to give me the same courtesy they had given him. He went back to the airport and flew home to stay in the bed for weeks. *This was like the guy who burned all his ships on the enemy's shore and couldn't turn back. I had to make this thing work!* I remember thinking if I didn't stick with this gig, I would have to start all over again back in Chesapeake. That didn't fit too well.

I took the job for $900 per week plus expenses. It wasn't up to consultant fees, but it was a living at the time. Before long, I discovered that Bob's brother wasn't exactly treating the Charlotte branch fairly. He had bid a job in South Carolina using the Charlotte State licenses. Then he had the Charlotte branch pay all the payrolls and expenses for much of the materials for the project, but he ordered the payments for the job mailed to his branch office in Richmond, Virginia. In other words, the Charlotte branch of Dagenhart was bearing the brunt of the South Carolina expenses and the income was going into his Richmond Virginia account. Rather than bother a sick man, I drove to South Carolina, flashed my business card as being an officer of the Charlotte Division and had them send the checks directly to the Charlotte office. All of a sudden, we had cash flow to cover some of the expenses. It took a while for the brother to realize he wasn't getting any more checks for his account. When he did realize this a few weeks later, he was not a happy camper. He wanted me gone, but couldn't tell Bob why. Frankly, I didn't care what he thought because I could not respect a man who would steal from his sick brother.

Then, I did an "In-house Chapter 11". Listing all the creditors and the amounts owed, I did a cash flow projection of when I expected money to come in. We then used that cash flow income to make partial payments to each creditor over ten months time. Most of the creditors "went along to get along" due to Dagenhart's reputation. I had to convince the others if they resisted this plan, the company would go bankrupt and they would get nothing. It was time to play hardball and do the best for both Dagenhart and the creditors.

The two young men Glenn and Ken were invaluable. They pitched in and it was remarkable what they accomplished. Before long, we had some control. Then, with Glenn's help we set up a marketing scheme to service existing fire systems regularly, which led to our being asked to bid on several apartments during the rush of the apartment boom. After we were low bidder, Glenn and I lobbied the city to accept plastic pipe over copper, which would give us a better margin. By September 1994, the future looked a little brighter for the Charlotte operation.

Of course I knew that blood was thicker than water and I also knew that Bob's brother hated the ground I walked on. They had 15,000 square feet of warehouse and office space and only needed maybe 5,000 of it. I was blessed to rent the old one to a French firm with a long-term lease and then sell it, putting money back into Dagenhart rather than losing the building. Bob was thankful and relieved and his brother was just angry. They were on the verge of foreclosure unless the Dagenharts invested a lot of money to keep the division afloat.

We rented a smaller place in Northern Charlotte and as the year ended, I wanted to get back into business for myself. I talked to another friend named Jim Atwell and told him of the situation. I asked him if he would back me financially to purchase the Charlotte office of Dagenhart. He agreed and so

I made an offer, but nothing I offered was good enough for Bob's brother. By September of that year, Mary and I had sold our home in Chesapeake and paid off any and all obligations we had due to the Obenauer debacle. It was a good feeling. We had no debt. We also had no money.

It was interesting for me to observe closely how someone ran their business. Each month, I had to do many analyses for Bob and his brother. I soon saw two different management styles. Bob was smart and a very personable guy. I visited him in his Norfolk office as he recovered from his illness and it was neat to watch him operate. He was an exhorter. He would call in his various foremen, and list each project on a large board. He would look at what they had accomplished on each contract to date and decide how much revenue each of those foremen were to generate on their job over the next four weeks. He would have his bookkeeper monitor them weekly and would follow up weekly. I saw how he built such a successful operation.

However, his Achilles heel was ignoring what was going on in Charlotte, and also with his brother's operation in Richmond. He was wealthy, receiving a lot of income from his real estate rentals and he was too sick to face his brother. I tendered my resignation because I did not want to deal with Bob's brother, and Bob's brother took over the Charlotte operation. Glenn and Ken left almost immediately, and the operation closed down. Everything was moved from Charlotte to Richmond after I left. The good news was, they did not owe everybody in Charlotte.

What did I learn? I believe I confirmed what I already knew down inside—that I knew how to turn a business around and manage people. Sometimes that will give you a big boost.

· I learned no matter how profitable a company had been, without weekly or monthly controls it can get so far out of hand it will go broke and no one will know why. Whatever you're your style is, without numbers, you will fail. (My daughter Susan tells me accounting is the language of business... I think she is right.)

· I affirmed what I had learned previously from dealing with my own creditors. It pays to keep creditors informed. Creditors absolutely love to have someone tell them something. Those who were ready to file suits for collections became interested partners instead of adversaries. Any management style that does not include honesty and integrity is due for a fall if creditors get a whiff of it.

· I learned that my style of communication with my employees was in line with what Bob did with his own successful operations. If you don't target and make projections, you will not accomplish goals. You have to give people a goal and hold them accountable. If they don't have a clear picture of what you think they must accomplish, they won't try. I had done that with Glenn and Ken in Charlotte and they were the ones who really saved that company. All I did was rally them, give them daily and weekly goals with a one year plan, and they marched toward it in spite of the difficulties.

· *I learned that I wasn't a failure as much as I thought.* I had witnessed a bonafide business turnaround and with God's help, I had been the one driving the train.

· Most of all I learned what has turned out to be true time after time. During the first phase of consulting everyone loves you. When the operation becomes successful and is no longer a threat, you remind the owners that they failed at it, so they don't want you there to remind them of their mistakes. That's just the way it is.

In September of 1994 (about three months before the Charlotte operation came to a close), Mary and I had agreed on prayers backed by Scripture. We printed them out and used the prayers as a daily confession. The daily confession built our faith and they all have come to pass. We were living in Charlotte in a rented condominium with our daughter Ashley. I was sixty-one years old and the devil was screaming inside my head that *"you are too old to do anything except retire." "Nobody wants to hire a has-been" "Look at you, you are a total failure. How are you going to look after Mary and Ashley? Why don't you just give up?"*

Those thoughts were magnified when it became apparent that Bob's brother would not sell any part of the business to me because I had nailed him in front of his brother over his capture of the company's funds. By December of that year, it was evident that soon I had better find employment and find a way to continue my climb back out of the mess we were in. I had a good reputation with banks from Chesapeake to Charlotte, but no collateral.

In our prayer confessions, we prayed, believed we received and began to thank God for three basic things over our finances. All three prayers were answered before the times requested.

1. By December 31, 1994, I would have a good job producing abundant income. (Based on III John 1:2-"Father we thank you that we are going to prosper and be in health, even as our souls prosper.")

2. By December 31, 1998, we would have a home with at least $150,000 equity in it. (Based on Romans 13:8- "Father thank you we are to owe nobody anything but

love for one another.")

3. By December 31, 2000. we would have a home paid for
    and at least $100,000 saved. (Based on Proverbs 13:22-
    "Father, we thank you for our leaving an inheritance
    to our grandchildren and the wealth of the sinner is
    laid up for the just.")

It looked like the prayer for having a job producing income was not going to be realized until 30th of December, 1994,
the day before our goal. *Did you ever notice how it seems God
will wait to see if you really have faith?* I received a phone call
from Jim Atwell, Owner and President of Atwell Industries.
Atwell invented and produced the "Tuffliner" pickup truck
plastic bed for every make imaginable. I had known him since
Rock Church where we both served on the Washington for Jesus
Campaign. He was also the man who had enough faith in me
to back me on the purchase of the Dagenhart Charlotte operation.

He was having a big problem with his National Marketing
Manager. I drove to his home in Greenville, NC on the night of
December 31, 1994 and was hired as a consultant to revamp
his Marketing operation. I spent the night in his home, know-
ing that God had honored our prayer and had "cut it close"
just to let me know He was in charge. I woke up on New Year's
Day in his home and went to work in his office on that day.
That was my job by December 31, 1994 we had prayed for.

It didn't take long to see this was an interesting assign-
ment. I learned a lot. Jim had set up a series of retail outlets
in many states to sell his own product. He had been forced to
do that due to his competition, which seemed to have a pretty
good stronghold on individual car/truck dealerships, auto
stores, garages, etc. He had continued to boost his production
by hiring individual retail salesmen who would rent a warehouse, order direct from his factory in Greenville, NC and stock-
pile the needs for every dealership and retail outlet in their

area. It proved profitable and allowed his new factory to produce a lot of products. After a while though, he began to realize that many of the salesmen were falsifying their warehouse
inventory and were selling units installed on the side and stick-
ing the money in their pockets. My job was to (1) root them
out and (2) find out an alternative plan.

I will not go into all the details, but it was an interesting
year. I had to confront angry salespeople whom I had caught
red handed. Some of them were not very friendly, particularly,
one we called the "alligator man" in Baton Rouge, LA. I
thought I was going to wind up as alligator bait, but when I
confronted him with facts in a motel room at 8 o'clock one
night, he cried like a baby. *I surely did pray for favor and protec-
tion before the six foot three inch tall alligator man came to my
room that night to turn in his keys and records.* Another salesman in Fort Worth, Texas threatened to work me over. I was
told he was a former football player for the Philadelphia Eagles.
I had such a high fever from the flu while firing him in the rain
that day, it would have been an easier way to get through the
day if he had knocked me out, but thank God he didn't. He
finally surrendered his keys and his records.

Jim and I worked out a national strategy that worked by
breaking up the country in regions and hiring regional salespeople who did not threaten each other and who sold directly
to outlets where we could "drop ship" truckloads of products
and collect within 30 days. He kept a few of his local salesmen, but very few. They were in isolated areas that did not
cross his area sales people.

I was fascinated by Jim's management style, because it
was so different from mine. I knew he had been extremely successful in manufacturing and selling his product. He was very
profit oriented and was one of the most secretive people I had
ever met. I guess it would be fair to say that we had two distinct different personalities. My style was to lay all the facts

on the table, to bring in those working with me to look at them, agree on a strategy to change things, and then hold everyone accountable before the next meeting.

With customers, I would do the same thing. I would listen to an idea or complaint, make an immediate decision and come up with a plan to follow. Not only that, but I would put it in writing. I could see that those people at Atwell really ate it up and began to rally around everything I was doing. The production picked up and Jim asked me to help organize the factory.

Immediately, I found those who wanted to improve and began to set up meetings on Saturdays. My criteria was that those who were not interested enough to come to a company paid breakfast would be remembered when promotions and raises were handed out. To be more specific, if they weren't interested enough to come to a free breakfast, I wasn't interested in giving them any promotions. The factory leaders bought it quickly. They saw it as a direct contrast to the way Jim operated. Which was to look from his office window with a one way glass at what they were doing and only communicate when he wanted or needed something.

His style was to work as few hours as he had to, to put pressure on everyone he dealt with. He trusted his Controller and lived by the numbers. If the numbers said we were not making the kind of profits we should, more pressure would come down to the workers and salesmen. You know what? It worked. I should have noticed more.

My style was to work from morning until night and beyond if we had something to do. I remember leaving Dallas, Texas one morning at 5 o'clock and driving within two hours of the office in Greenville, NC before I stopped for the night, so I could get up and in the office the next day. I wasn't but sixty-two years old then. As far as I was concerned, I was still a young man.

I was just plain ignorant of the fact that Jim didn't like my management style. I should have taken the hint when Jim had a personality test for all of us. It showed me as an ESTP, or one who is an extrovert, sensitive, thoughtful and percep-tive. Jim was an ISTJ, which meant he was an introvert, sen-sitive, thoughtful and judgmental. We were set for a clash and I didn't have enough sense to see it coming.

One night I was working in the office and I received a phone call from Jim. He and his wife Barbara were on their way to dinner and he said to me, "I see you are still working. That makes me feel very uncomfortable." I was surprised, but kept right on working. I never was good at taking a hint when I was busy doing something. I like to call it focus, but I'm not sure that's best in all circumstances.

Picture this: Here was a very rich guy, very successful who micro managed when he thought he should and stayed away when he should. Here I was, working for him trying to do things my way and even though I was having success, it was like throwing cold water in his face. *I have never been very good at recognizing things politically.* My Myers-Briggs test had dubbed me as "The Ultimate Realist." To me whatever it took to do the job, as long as it was honest, was all I needed to think about. *So much for Myers-Briggs opinions.*

We parted ways and he treated me with a lot of dignity, and I came away learning a few things.

1. No matter how successful you are at what you are do-ing, if someone else has the authority and he also has his money in a venture, do not confront him with your attitude and actions. It is bad for the company, for the two of you and those who work there. *That goes for anyone furnishing the money in any venture you are in-volved with.*

2.   His style worked good for his personality. His workers were some of the best paid and the best treated in the entire area. His bonus plans were good, his intent was good and he did his best to get respect by being like he was.

3.   Jim and Barbara were born again Spirit filled Christians and God made them with different personalities than Mary and I. I had to learn to respect that and not cram my style down his throat. My style was to be open and communicate my expectations, while Jim's was to just let them know his expectations through his actions.

4.   He did the important things. He wasn't interested in a "feel good" place; he was interested in an efficient place. He knew where he stood as to costs and profits as well as anyone I know and he did all those things that are smart.

5.   Where my style was to strap on my six guns and go "ready, fire, aim", Jim would strategize something until I was bored. You know what? We were both right. What works for me would not work for him and vice versa. I used to wonder why it took him so long to make up his mind while he thought I was being presumptuous by going from my gut. We both usually came to the same conclusion in the end. We just approached each problem differently and processed things differently.

6.   The bottom line was, they tithed and gave more into the Kingdom of God financially than I did at that particular time. His style was good for him and it caused him to be successful.

CONCLUSIONS:

· Each of us should learn how to maximize our profits using our own style. Some of us do it through communication and expectation.

· Some of us do it just by letting everyone know we have expectations without the communications. (I know that is not the new model for success, but frankly, it works for a lot of people in business.) The downside is no one knows what to expect, but the upside is the employees continue to try and please because they do not want to fail, so production is accomplished.

· Some of us work hard at communication and try to have a workplace that "every one feels like a team member." That is good when it works, but when team members think it means they can let things slide, it works against you. I will take expectations over communications, any day.

· Remember, when someone (they can be Christians, liberals, or anyone who has never had to meet a payroll weekly) keeps telling you that the "working model is entrepreneurial partnerships in the workplace," prayerfully look at each of your workers and decide which ones will take advantage of that prior to your doing it. It sounds good, but seldom works in a small business setting; even though that is my honest hearts desire to see it work. It will work with one or two confidants, but will not work with everyone.

- Finally, understand that those nice sounding modern day models of human resource relationships are primarily for big corporations. There is no doubt that "partnership" styles work in a massive setting. When you have a small business with say, ten people you, the business owner, are at the core. If two of those employees take advantage of your allowing them to be "free spirits" your operation will fail. Use your style to get to the bottom line. Be fair, be honest and it is perfectly alright to be demanding. If the employees don't like it, allow them to work elsewhere.

- There is a lot of merit to delegating authority. However, I have found that delegating without following up to see what the person is accomplishing is a guarantee for problems. Once in a while you can find someone who will accept a large mantel of responsibility. When you find that person, reward him/her, but have some method of holding them accountable. Otherwise you will wake up disappointed.

- I would like to believe all you have to do is hire Christians to fill your positions of major responsibility. That is not necessarily true. Hire competent Christians if you can, but be sure they understand what you expect from them. What they expect to give in time and effort and what you expect could be worlds apart.

- Whatever your management style may be, <u>know what it is</u>. Know your strengths and know your weaknesses. Utilize your strengths, and look for someone who is strong in areas you are weak, but don't allow them to know that you know the difference.

Finally, if you are not a numbers person, get someone who is whom you trust totally. Your management style must include details. *I have never met a successful businessperson who didn't know what his numbers were and what his competition was doing.* Without that, you are fighting in the dark.

WHAT IS CHAPTER FOUR ALL ABOUT?

1. A management style must include having:
_____or _____controls.

2. A management style that does not include
_____and _____is due for a fall if it is in
debt to several creditors and they get a whiff of it.

3. If your employees don't have a clear picture of what you
think the must accomplish, they won't _____.

4. If you are a manager who has superiors and though you
are very successful, should you confront those who have the
authority and investment if they don't agree with your
style? Yes_____ No_____.

5. Which is most important to a business? A "feel good"
place or one that is profitable? _____
_____.

6. Is maximizing your style through communication and
expectation a good thing? Yes_____ No_____.

7. The downside of managing expectations without communications is _____
_____but the upside is
_____.

8. Delegating without follow up is a guarantee
_____.

9. Be sure when you hire someone they are told what is _____ of them. Their idea may be worlds apart from yours.

10. When you know what your management style is with its strengths and weakness, hire someone that has _____ in areas you are _____.

11. In order to be successful, regardless of your style you need to know two things. Your _____ and your _____.

5 | Watch Out When Dealing With "The Big Boys"

Don't associate with evil men; don't long for their favors and gifts. Their kindness is a trick; they want to use you as their pawn. [Proverbs 23:6 TLB]

I knew God was working in our lives. Mary and I agreed that we would "wait on God" before the next move. The Atwell's had been gracious to pay me for my services through the entire year in 1995, even though I wound up my activities there in August. Frankly, we had accomplished all that Jim and I set out to do by that time and it was time for me to move on.

Mary and I agreed that we would pray daily about our next move until we both heard from the Holy Spirit. It was a long August. Finally, we both said we believed that God had revealed what we were to do. I wanted to go back to Charlotte where I saw loads of contacts and opportunities. I remembered the Obenauer ordeal and just sat tight, because I did not want to make a move due to economic necessity from a lack of faith. Finally, we sat down and wrote down what we believed God had shown us.

1. Move back to Graham, NC and look after my mom and dad. My mom had fallen and broken her pelvis and Dad

had a cornea operation on both eyes that didn't work too well. (That was the last thing I *wanted* to do, but I realized we should.)

2. Look for an opportunity as a consultant, but keep my eyes open for opportunities besides just a job.

3. Go to a church that God would reveal to us after we moved.

By October 2, 1995 we packed up our belongings once again, put them in a 48 foot storage trailer and moved into a 1300 square foot house beside my parent's home. It was evident why God had sent us back to Graham. Even though we visited regularly and tried to see to my parents' needs were met, they had done a pretty good job of covering up the fact that they really needed daily care.

Mary was a jewel. She pitched in and began to spoil them so much with cooking, cleaning and taking care of them, I told her within a few weeks she had better slow down or she was setting a precedent that would be hard to keep up. Of course, she paid no attention, she just barreled ahead and within a few months, I began to wonder if my parents weren't in better health than either of us.

Within three weeks, Ronnie Kirkpatrick owner of Triangle Grading & Paving, Inc. hired me as a Vice President and CEO. His company was billing about $19,000,000 per year in highway, water and sewer, paving and concrete work. His goal was to grow it to $30,000,000 in three years. We were able to do that and more. In fact, within three years, we had it up to $33,000,000 and I was almost burned out. Ronnie had less communication skills than Jim Atwell, but he too was extremely successful. Of course, he overcame every obstacle in his way by working seven days per week, every week, and every year. However, it had cost him a marriage and a close relationship with some of his family. I liked him and appreciated the fact that he was a worker.

By mid 1998, Mary and I already had our new home overlooking two ponds and with God's help and direction, had met our other financial goals. I had spent eleven months back in Charlotte cleaning up a $11,000,000 mess that one of Triangle's Division Managers had created. During that stint, I had been given the title of "President of the Charlotte Division." It was evident the Charlotte Division needed to be closed and moved back into the central headquarters in Burlington, NC.

When I returned, Ronnie had hired a young man whom I had sued for fraud years earlier in Chesapeake, VA. Ronnie liked him; he was years younger than me, very knowledgeable with computers and cost accounting. Obviously, though he and I were cordial to each other, there was too much water over the dam for us to get along very well. Besides, I decided that Ronnie would figure him out sooner or later. At the same time, after all the Charlotte work, I was ready to calm down and do something else, so I turned in my thirty-day notice. Of course, Ronnie had been good as his word to me. When I had agreed to go to Charlotte, he agreed to build an eighteen hundred foot road on my lot and build a pond in front of my new house. Triangle furnished most of the equipment and I handled the operations on the weekends. Even though Ronnie had done all of that, I knew it was time for me to make a change. I was not going to wind up a subordinate to a younger guy I thought was dishonest.

It was the year of my dad's 90th birthday. My mom was 84. Mary had her hands full with both of them as well as our youngest daughter Ashley, who was 16 years old with all the typical teen age problems and then some.

Even while I was working my notice for Triangle I received a phone call from a young man named Marion Waters. He was an accountant who graduated from NC State and I had hired him as a new controller in 1996 at Triangle. When I left for Charlotte, he and Ronnie did not see eye to eye, so he left. He had worked with an international drug manufacturer and had left them to become controller of a small cable construction company in Durham, NC named Winn Caribe of NC.

Marion asked me to meet with his company president, Joe Marceno. He said that the little company had been doing two to three million dollars per year, but was on the verge of taking contracts to build Cable TV systems for Time Warner that would approach twelve million dollars the next year.

I remember thinking that helping them build a company almost from scratch would be exciting. I thought it would be a welcome change to work with the "big boys" (Time Warner and others their size) and wondered how far up the corporate ladder I could establish relationships with those who ran those national cable networks. *I remember thinking, "I have spent my life working with locals; I wonder what it would be like going toe to toe with the big boys?"*

I met with Marion and Joe Marceno and was totally unimpressed. They had an office warehouse located on Alston Avenue in Durham. While we met, people continued to run from the warehouse into the office. I got the feeling that this place was totally disorganized. Marion's office was a small closed-in box at one end of the tiny office. Joe's place was even worse. It was about the size of a big walk-in closet and he shared it with a happy, plump African-American woman named Shirley, who was the sole payroll clerk and secretary.

Somehow, we continued to talk over the next few weeks, and finally I told them that I could write them a business plan that looked good, but it wouldn't be worth much without implementation. Furthermore, I told them that I knew how to organize people and set up systems, but I knew nothing about TV cable or telephone businesses. *In fact, I didn't want*

91

to know much, because when someone started telling me about megahertz, my eyes would glaze over.

Finally, Joe made me a proposition. He had a project manager who was working his notice on a project in Goldsboro, NC, and he asked me if I would go there and take over the project. He would assign a person who knew all about the cable construction part, if I would organize the warehouse controls, set up safety programs they did not have, hire and fire as I needed to prepare his group for the growth that was yet to come. I believed my past experience had taught me just how to do that.

I found it a fascinating proposition. By October, I had turned sixty-six years old, so what the heck. I rented an apartment in Goldsboro, working in Winn Caribe's office there, and began the organizational trek that pulled the company together. I work out a needs analysis for the company and focused on ten things detrimental to their growth and profit. I stayed there until February 1999.

There were four owners. Joe was president, Kevin Winn, who lived in Texas, was Vice President; Ace Olsofsky lived in Puerto Rico along with the fourth partner, Peter Gillis. All four had begun as cable jockeys and had met during a hurricane in Puerto Rico, and even though Ace and Kevin had their own companies, they formed Winn Caribe. (Winn Communications + Caribe Communications equaled Winn Caribe to them).

By the end of 1998, the company had performed $4.7 million dollars in contracts. In the meantime, I had set up controls, maintenance, accountability, and safety programs; and in February 1999, they promptly gave me a ticket to Barbados for a board meeting where they offered me the position of CEO. I accepted by faith. They were a group of hard drinking, hard living guys whose main interest was making money.

We had an agreement that any changes I proposed for the

company would be agreed to by the majority of the four. Once they agreed on the concept or challenge, I would have complete authority to make those changes and hold accountable any party that was responsible for any failure or slack. It worked like a charm. Of course, some of it was because times were good in that industry. There was so much more work to be done in the cable, phone, and internet industry and there simply weren't enough good contractors to go around. It was a contractor's market.

One of the things that concerned me was the fact that Winn Caribe had only one major customer. It was Time Warner. That is always dangerous. So, I set out to acquire more customers. In fact, by early 1999, the partners were sure we would have to become subcontractors rather than prime contractors. I did not believe that, so I set out to get our name in the pot with the big boys.

In the meantime, the partners agreed to have Winn Caribe buy out Kevin and Joe's company, WinnComm and make Kevin our Western VP. Before the end of 1999, we had a $4,000,000 job in Boston with Cablevision, our work in North Carolina, and $2,000,000 in contracts with Cox Communications in Texas as well as work in Virginia with Adelphia. That year the little company did over $13,000,000 in revenues and had about 12% profit before taxes. I kept pushing for work throughout the United States and soon Kevin, Ace, and Joe were busy as beavers looking after the day to day operations. It was fun to find the headquarters of one of the "big boys" and learn a way to get to whoever had the authority to contract with Winn Caribe. At times, I would begin with the Chairman's office, who would then tell me who to call. I would then call that person with the introduction that the Chairman said to call him about bidding on any future work he had in his division. That usually got a response from the person I wanted to talk to.

The partners were gracious to both Marion and I, paying

us handsome bonuses along with our salaries. The partners then began to grumble among themselves. Some of them wanted to bleed the cash as soon as it came in while Joe wanted desperately to grow the company. My loyalty was to Joe, and I found an ally in Ace. Finally in a board meeting in the fall of 1999, I told them that they needed to either decide who wanted to be bought out or who wanted to sell, but I was not interested in this undercurrent of fighting among them. They authorized me to find a buyer. I did and by April 25th, 2000 Corenet Services, Inc. of Atlanta, Georgia had purchased Winn Caribe of NC, Inc. for a purchase price of $13,000,000. About one third of the purchase was cash, another third was based upon numbers of revenue and profit by year's end, and the other 40% was to be in Corenet stock.

We blew the numbers away that year, because Winn Caribe Communications (the new acquired company name) did $22,400,000 in 2000 and had another stellar year of 12% profits before taxes. Things looked good.

My life consisted of flying somewhere two or three days per week. I became the liaison person between Winn Caribe and Corenet, as well as continuing to set up meetings and push for new clients in the new locations. In 2001, we did $35,100,000 in volume and 11% profit before taxes. Dealing with the "big boys" was fun. They needed us and we all worked hard to be the best at what we did. Soon, we had projects in Simi Valley California, Georgia, New York, Virginia, North Carolina, and I was working on Salt Lake City with AT&T.

Things began to go sour at Corenet. Corenet had been organized by a reverse merger with a company from Greensboro, NC called Network Construction Services, Inc. Corenet had hired a professional CEO to deal with New York banks to buy out smaller companies and to become "infrastructure service providers." That was a fancy name for outside and inside plant contractors to perform work for telephone and cable companies, inside wiring for places like CNN in Atlanta, and to string cable on poles or underground anywhere in the nation. One of the Corenet companies was an engineering company that provided the design for much of the work, so there were four of us to perform the work. It seemed like a good plan. Five companies owned by a parent company that could provide it all.

Corenet had borrowed $38,000,000 from Duestchebank and another $11,000,000 from Mellon Bank. By the end of year 2000, they had paid all but $1,400,000 to the partners of Winn Caribe for the stock purchase. It became obvious to me that they did not have the ready cash to pay the balance, so after consulting with Joe, Kevin, and Ace, I wrote them a letter, placing them on notice that, according to the agreement, they owed us the money by year's end. (The partners had given Marion and I five percent each of the company stock, so the $6,000,000 cash would have been a blessing to us all.)

That was a strange position for me to be in. On one hand, I represented our team of the four original partners, Marion and myself. On the other hand, I was CEO of a wholly owned Corenet company and had to keep good relations with the people for whom I was directly working.

I really enjoyed the relationships with the CEOs and operations people with our other four subsidiaries. It was a real eye opener for me to see though, how little control the parent company had over the subsidiaries, and how out-of-control some of the subsidiaries were. There was no one with the parent company directing the ship. All Corenet seemed to be interested in was getting on the Stock Exchange and going public.

The first casualty was a company in Florida that was purchased by Corenet just prior to Winn Caribe being purchased. The president was an egotistical fellow and always claimed his work was making more profit than it was. Before I knew what was going on, I received a call from the treasurer of Corenet.

He told me the board had dismissed the Florida company's president, and he asked me to go there, clean out his office, fire or hire his people, and for Winn Caribe to take over his equipment and finish the jobs he had in Florida and New York. That was a challenge. Joe pitched in and so did Jon Baranosky, a fellow I had hired from Time Warner. It took a few months to make that transition.

Next, the president of Network Construction was fired (at the direction of Duestchebank I was told) and I was asked to go to Greensboro and do the same thing I had done in Florida. That was in early 2002 and things really got sideways. Corenet had hired a new COO to take over Network's operation nationwide. He lived in California, had his main office in Greensboro and all of the company's work was in Des Moines, Iowa, Seattle, Washington and Denver, Colorado. Network Construction Services was in a mess. Its books were all out of whack and I sensed a huge loss coming soon. The trouble was, it took weeks to get a handle on the numbers. I knew the results were bad, but didn't know how bad.

Next, the banks forced the board of Corenet to fire the CEO of Corenet. They hired a temporary person, who was a real gentleman. His name was Jerry Gurbacki and his claim to fame was that he was president of a national linen service company. He asked me to meet him in Denver to go over the Network situation. There, Network Construction was working strictly for Qwest. I was shocked out of my mind when I began to appraise that situation.

Network had millions of dollars under contract, but they had crews leave their $9,000 per month office and warehouse yard complex, and travel to all points north, south, east and west of Denver placing DSL systems for internet service. I could not tell by their books and records in Greensboro how much money they were losing each month, but I decided to stay in Denver until I found out.

First, I discovered they had two project managers, which meant no one was responsible. When something went wrong, it was the other guy's fault. Secondly, no one tried to match their billings to Qwest with the numbers reported in Greensboro. Furthermore, the Profit and Loss statements in Greensboro reflected the *cost of each item performed* by the company *plus its anticipated profit.* In other words, whatever it was costing to perform the work, Network's books reflected they were making their mark-up anticipated as profit. *What a way to go broke in a hurry!* They had no way of knowing what the real cost was.

My first decision was to ask for an organization chart so I could determine who was doing what. I made that request of both "project managers" as well as the Denver engineer. Guess what? They came up with three different organizational charts.

The Denver office had almost 100 employees, so I laid off 40% of the workers at one swoop. Production rose 50% the next week. People were punching in at the shop, riding around to heaven knows where and punching back out at night.

Here we were, losing money at a rate that could choke a horse, hearing that Qwest was on the verge of Chapter 11, owing Network $3.2 million dollars and I had to somehow get that money into Corenet's (or Deustchebank's) coffers and tell Qwest that we were going to stop working at the same time. Talk about praying, I did a bunch of it.

I asked my son Jack III to help me. He was a great help. We learned that Network had another office in Des Moines with several vehicles, bucket trucks, and backhoes, and was paying $4,000 per month for an office/warehouse that hadn't been active for months. No one in the home office was aware of it. They had a project manager in Des Moines on payroll that no one in Greensboro knew about. They thought he was another "project manager" in Denver. Jack III went to Des Moines with about $5,000 cash in his pockets and hired everybody he could off the streets who had drivers license to help ferry all that equipment to Denver. It took him several days and he didn't have much time. The owner of the yard in Des Moines had confronted him about Network's delinquency in payment of rent and told Jack he and his wife was going to Europe for a week and that Jack "had better have the money for the rent by the time they returned." He threatened to have the yard locked down by the local sheriff. Jack III called me and said, "Dad, we had better get out of Dodge." I sent him the cash and he did, driving night and day with whomever he could hire and keep sober enough to get between Des Moines and Denver.

I made a couple of trips to the Des Moines area when I found out several of the TV cable owners, all clients of Network, owed Network, but Network owed subcontractors just as much. The cable owners wanted to release the money, but had to get everyone to agree to lien releases, so that made for several meetings with disgruntled people who had dealt with Network. The trouble was, Network had bonded some of the jobs, and it either had to be settled or Corenet and the bank would face a fight with the bonding companies. After several negotiations, it was settled and the money released.

The next turn was to sell about $2,000,000 of Network equipment as well as tell lenders who were owed balances on another $4,000,000 in Network equipment loans they were not going to get paid. Most of them wanted us to have a sale and send them the proceeds while others just got nasty. The sale took place on the Denver yard and anything that wasn't sold was moved back to North Carolina. The owner of the yard that Network leased had the sheriff place attachments on some of the vehicles for local debts owed by Network, so we left them. Better to get 95% of the pie than nothing.

The $3.2 million owed to Network by Qwest was compounded by the same problem. Suppliers and subs were owed just as much. There were seventy-three irate subs and suppliers who demanded their money. Jack III and I came up with a plan to satisfy them as well as we could. One by one, they signed off and we finally got Qwest to place its $3.2 million in a Lawyers Title Trust Account in Chicago until we could get everyone signed off. Basically, we got everyone to accept about sixty four cents on the dollar. If we hadn't worked like dogs, they would have gotten nothing. So, Lawyers Title dispersed $2.7 million to the vendors and subs and we were able to hand $500,000 over to the bank on behalf of Corenet. That year ended and I was exhausted, trying to look after Winn Caribe on the fly while curing problems from Florida to Denver. Meanwhile, Qwest had its CEO dismissed under a cloud of reporting false numbers to Wall Street. I looked for it to file for Chapter 11, but thankfully they reorganized on their own behalf.

In the midst of the entire trauma, I met one of the most astute, honest and reliable men I have ever met. His name was Anthony Aliamo from Peachtree City, Georgia. He was a consultant for the bank. In the beginning, little did I know that he had been charged by Duestchebank to walk into Corenet, make an assessment of the situation and then bankrupt the whole mess. Anthony was smart enough to see that the bank would be better served to close out Network, let Winn Caribe absorb what was left of the Florida operation as well as Network's and sell the three remaining companies.

Like most of life, things were bittersweet. On one hand I could see my employment was coming to an end, sooner or later. On the other hand, I was operating in the "Big Corporate World" and fullfilling some of my dreams. Frankly, I was a little amazed at how things operated on a national level. Big business was the same as little business. If the outgo was more than the income, the business failed. It just took longer to get a handle on major issues. I also felt a great deal of satisfaction that my past had taught me how to react to problems. It was as if all the hard times in the past had taught me what to do every moment. I prayed and the Holy Spirit directed me. At times, it was a lot of fun to cure problems, *especially when it wasn't my money invested in the venture.*

Before I knew it, Anthony and I were like two gloves on two hands. He was the direct liaison with the bank and I was the operations guy making it happen on the ground. When I needed authorization to do something, I justified it to him, and he, in turn, justified it with the bank. This was also the time that all the big dot com companies began to fall. The cable companies began to become slow pay. Cash flow became worse. Then Winn Caribe's balance sheet took a tremendous hit. Adelphia Communications Corporation owed us over $6,000,000 and they made excuses week after week as to why they did not pay while demanding we finish projects in California, Virginia and Florida.

I contacted Anthony and Jim True, President of our sister company, True Engineering. Adelphia owed Jim's company another $1,000,000. If Adelphia fell, Corenet would take a $7,000,000 hit. That would be a major body blow. It was early 2002, and Winn Caribe had a good project going for AT&T in Salt Lake City, Utah as well as projects in Texas and Arkansas for Cox Communications whose headquarters for that area was in Tyler, Texas. Could we survive by keeping our forces going on the good jobs to carry the slow paying ones? That was the question.

Adelphia Communications Corporation was headquartered in a small western Pennsylvania town called Coudersport. It was nestled between rolling mountains and was definitely a place that "you had to go somewhere else to get there." There were no airports nearby, so on Monday afternoon, May 13, 2002 Anthony, Jim and I caught a plane to Elmira, NY. We rented a four wheel SUV and drove over the winding roads to Coudersport. Knowing we were coming unannounced, we wondered just what we would accomplish.

I was sure of one thing. We would not leave without talking to someone to give us an idea of what was going on in the Adelphia headquarters. Earlier I had spoken to a wonderful pastor in Coudersport whom I had met through Rock Church. He had given me some news that helped motivate me to get there in a hurry. The news on the street in Coudersport was that Mr. John Rigas, founder and CEO, was in emergency meetings. It was all over the *Wall Street Journal* that Adelphia was having trouble verifying its 2001 report to the SEC, and that auditors were flooding the corporate offices. The trade journals had always touted John Rigas as a "self made man" and with his two sons, Timothy and Michael, he had built quite a fortune by buying up smaller cable systems and making them into one big one. They had systems in the Northeast, Southeast and in California as well as Puerto Rico.

When I asked my pastor friend what did the "word on the street" have to say about their financial stability, he said, "Jack, Mr. Rigas is a multi-millionaire, but before his two sons took over he was a billionaire." That was not good news, especially with Winn Caribe performing about $600,000 per week in contract work for them at the time.

I had made a trip about three months earlier and collected money Adelphia owed us, but the balance was getting out of hand. I found the people in Coudersport to be good, reliable hard working western Pennsylvania people and I could tell by talking to them over the phone as well as from my previous visit that all was not going well. We arrived in Coudersport about twilight and checked in to a local motel. I waited for my friend's call, and sure enough he agreed to meet with us at his church about 9:00 A.M. the next morning. Just before he hung up the phone he said, "We are holding a 5:00 A.M. prayer meeting and we will be praying for you." "Thanks," I said, knowing we would need all the help we could get.

The next morning, we were given the usual hangouts for Mr. Rigas including where he ate lunch each day. We decided to find his office and proceed. His office was not in the big elaborate headquarters building perched high overlooking the town, but he had bought an old school building downtown near City Hall. Parking in front on the busy morning street, we walked in as wide eyed as a calf looking at a new gate. As we walked down the hall from the entrance we could see scores of accountants busy with ledgers and adding machines. I would guess there was 20-30 of them crowded into what used to be school rooms. Suddenly we were at the end of the hallway, so we turned and walked upstairs. There were walking into John Rigas' secretary's office sitting at her desk asking what she could do for us.

Looking to our left was a big open glassed office and I could recognize the much published face of Mr. Rigas along with several other men. His face seemed flushed and it seemed as if several people were having much to say. Again, the secretary asked, "What can we do for you?" I told her that we must see Mr. Rigas because if he didn't pay us the $7,000,000 owed to us we would have to declare bankruptcy ourselves. She wrote it on a notepad and asked us to take a seat in the waiting area.

After waiting about ten minutes, a young man named Michael Mulcahey came out to meet us. He was an assistant to Timothy Rigas. His eyes were red as if he had been up most of the night. I told him the same thing that we had told the secretary and I really appreciated what he said, while looking intensely with his tired eyes. "Mr. Rigas doesn't want to hurt anybody." When I told him we would continue working at the present rate if he would guarantee us checks amounting to about $600,000 per week and that we would apply them to the oldest invoices, he said, "You had better stop performing that much work per week." Then I knew we were in trouble. He said he would call his accounts payable department and

Winn Caribe could pick up a check along with True Engineering the next morning. We left Coudersport with a check for almost $600,000 paying old invoices and Jim had one for a little over $100,000.

We had breakfast the next morning and the news in the local paper was that Jim Rigas had resigned as CEO, but he was keeping a seat on the board. I guess that was what all the fuss was about the previous morning in his office. The whole town was sad, because Mr. Rigas was a local icon. The town almost held him in reverence, and according to those we talked to, a mighty giant had fallen.

Adelphia Communications Corporation was a real American business story that came true. John Rigas, at the time an electronics engineer, bought a local movie theater in Coudersport in 1951. The next year he purchased a failing cable company for $300, or the story goes, to kill his competition at the theater. He and his brother Gus borrowed heavily over the next few years and bought out several local cable companies, one by one. It was organized as Adelphia Communications in 1972 and in the roaring 1990s, it purchased Century Communications in California for $5.2 billion. It became a cable service provider located in 32 states, had telephony assets, a sports radio station, the Empire Network sports cable channel, owned property it developed in many locations as well as the Buffalo Sabres, a NHL franchise. By 2002, it was broke and its executives were indicted and sentenced in Federal Court. I was glad to see Michael Mulcahey was finally set free upon sentencing at the trial. John and Timothy Rigas were sentenced and the family was ruined. What a sad story. S*o this was big business, I thought*.

Of course when a tidal wave like that hits, it takes a lot of small boats with it. Winn Caribe had a net worth of about six million prior to the Adelphia bankruptcy. It was about net zero after that.

We continued the struggle because the bank wanted everything to stay afloat long enough for it to sell True Engineering and its remaining in-house company, which was finally accomplished by the fall of 2002. Winn Caribe was the only company left standing.

Over the next several months, in order to collect monies due, a lawsuit was filed against Comcast (who bought out the Salt Lake City project from AT&T), a long drawn out fight with Time Warner to collect what was due from their Myrtle Beach, SC operation and compromises galore until it was time to close out and move on.

The lesson I learned dealing with the "big boys" is this: When they have budget problems, you can't find anyone to talk to who is willing to make a decision. If their problems are severe enough, the very managers you are dealing with will either quit or be replaced. Then, you are always dealing with the new guy who wants to "sweep with a new broom" and his claim to fame is how little he has to pay you for what his company owes you. The new guy usually has no feelings or obligations for what his predecessors obligated the company to on your behalf. The more ruthless he is, the better he looks to his superiors, who after all, now see you as just a number to get off their balance sheets.

That experience taught me a lot. It truly did allow me to work and negotiate with officers high on the corporate ladder on the national scene. It was a little disappointing too. Remember when you were a kid and you thought people in high places of command and control (beginning with your parents) knew exactly what they were doing? Remember when you grew up and realized that no one seemed to know what they were doing? That was my basic experience with the big boys. Here are some observations.

· When a business is capitalized with stockholder's money, the managers worry more about what the company's stock is going to be worth each quarter instead of planning long range.

· Most big corporations don't have controls that allow them to see ahead if a cash flow crunch is at hand. They just borrow more money based on the corporation's net worth and take their time to work things out. A small business doesn't have that luxury. *If you are a small business depending on the big corporation's cash flow to pay you what it owes, you should realize that you are very vulnerable.*

· Most corporate officers at the highest level are more interested in their own welfare than the welfare of the company. Because they get so caught up in being written and talked about, and the pure imagery that keeps the company stock up, they tend to stop getting involved at the front line levels. *If your business is looking to a big corporation to provide your revenue, remember that the person representing the "front line" element for the big corporation will at times make decisions to keep the "imagery" intact even if it delays or stops payment to you. They might tell you they feel bad about it, but it is always things like "budget changes" or "company consolidations" that can tie up your money for months, even for years.*

· Of course, there are some CEOs who are very interested in how the organization works and they stand out. For example, Lowe's comes to mind. Like him or not, Donald Trump is a hands on guy. The CEO of Comcast seems to eat and sleep his business also. Lee Iacocca was such a manager. He turned around Chrysler and talked the government into helping him. He cared about the company and its employees, and he also cared about his customers, which is rare. We need more Lee Iacoccas in the business world today.

- Finally, I believe that if a CEO fails at a publicly owned business, he should not be given a golden parachute that will make him rich for the balance of his life. That is stone cold wrong. Yet, it is not uncommon for a stock exchange company to lose money, stop paying dividends to the shareholders, and for the sake of image, fires the CEO. The fired CEO cries all the way to the bank because he is able to cash in his stock options, take several million dollars in a "goodbye" bonus from his guilty board of directors, and many times hired back as a consultant to help with the transition. As I stated earlier in this chapter, when Mike Mulcahey told me that "Mr. Rigas didn't want to hurt anybody" I believed it was the truth. However, the $7,000,000 Adelphia owed Corenet was such a small part of the problem it could not be rectified.

If you are looking to a big corporation as a major customer who represents over 50% of your revenue, you are in trouble the minute they are in trouble.

WHAT IS CHAPTER FIVE ABOUT?

1. When a company such as Corenet borrows almost $50,000,000 from two banks, who has the *real* control of the corporation? _____

2. In your opinion, was it the Christian thing to do when Jack Bailey settled with Network's creditors for 84 cents on the dollar with the money owed by Qwest to Network, and then paid Duestchebank the $500,000 difference? Explain your answer:

_____

_____

_____.

3. Was it the "Christian" thing to do to move Network's equipment off the yard in Des Moines Iowa to Denver in order to have a big sale and unload a lot of Network's debt?

_____

_____What would have been the alternative? _____

_____

4. Should Jack have used his friendship with a local Pastor in Coudersport to get into John Rigas' office?
Yes_____ No _____Why?

_____

5. Had you rather have several customers or clients or one or two big corporate clients to do business with? Several_____ One or two_____
Why?_____

6. Would you treat the owner of a small business who owes your company money for services or supplies in the same manner you treat the manager of a stock exchange corporation? _____

Why?_____

7. Have you ever been guilty in worrying more about your company's image than its integrity? Yes_____

No_____

8. If your business failed quickly, what would be your priorities as you were riding it to the ground?

(Number by priority) Your employees _____Your customers _____Your creditors_____

Your Note holders _____ Your family _____

Your equipment _____Your Real Estate _____

Your Reputation _____ Your friends _____

6 Christ is King in the Kingdom of God
Cash is King in the Kingdom of Business

Wealth hastily gotten will dwindle, but he who gathers little by little will increase it. [Proverbs 3:11 RSV]

As a very young businessman I thought if I worked hard enough, made enough smart deals and stayed on top of my business, it would grow. When it did just that, I continued to plow all of it right back into the business. I did that over and over and by an early age had a sizeable net worth. The deals became bigger, the profits followed suit *and the risks grew greater.*

So, when I lost, I lost more than I ever thought I could lose. Let's face it, 95% of all businesses that get into trouble, *if they have capable management, could be saved if they had pockets deep enough.* Things change, markets change, prices change, people change, interest rates change, equipment changes, and the demand for your services change. *If you don't have cash enough to weather those changes, your lifestyle will change because your business will decline or fail.* Not only do you need money to make the change, but you also need money to carry any transition or diversification.

I have wished that my parents had taught me the value of tithing to myself as well as tithing to the church. (They weren't high on tithing to the church, either). In today's environment everybody seems to be living up to their maximum in everything: maximum in time, in relationships, in payments, in salaries, in workload, *and maximum in dollars earned.* Now, why is that the case?

We have been sold that the "American Dream" is to enjoy everything to the maximum. When troubles or changes come, we don't have much left to bridge the gap. Christians are especially vulnerable because we are taught to live by faith. That is surely the way to live spiritually, mentally and physically. *We are talking about living financially.* If I had a choice to live by faith or live by fear, certainly I would choose faith. *Nowhere do the Scriptures tell us to live foolishly.* In fact, they tell us the opposite.

Take a look in Proverbs 1:32: *For the turning away of the simple shall slay them and the prosperity of fools shall destroy them.* (KJV) *Don't be a fool. Don't get yourself destroyed.* Proverbs 2:11 says, *Discretion will preserve you, understanding will keep you.* (NKJV) The Scriptures admonish us to *Get wisdom, get understanding* in Proverbs 4:5 (NKJV). James, who was Jesus' half brother, had a pretty good take on things. He wrote, *Come now you who say, Today or tomorrow we will go to such and such a city, spend a year there, buy and sell and make a profit; whereas you do not know what will happen tomorrow.* [James 4:13-14 NKJV]

I am also convinced through my own experience and dealing with other Christians in business, that *if a believer is a big giver of his finances to the Kingdom of God, there are spiritual forces that will try to stop that.* I know that sounds foolish to an unbeliever, but those of you who have faced situations that look as if some giant scheme suddenly came against you or your business to stop that cash overflow, *you know exactly what I am saying.*

I can give you some examples. But before I do, I want to

go on record that *when that happens, don't stop giving.* You might have to rethink how, when or what you give, but *don't stop giving.* I know because Mary and I have always followed that practice and we have always weathered the storm. *We have always come out on top!*

While writing this chapter, I was prompted to call one of my best Christian friends named Dick Hudson. He, his wife and family own Hudson Building Supply in Virginia Beach, VA. When I asked him for some examples of how he had experienced what I am now writing about, he began to chuckle. He said, "Jack, each time we make a pledge or commitment to give into the Kingdom, we can expect to have everything, including the kitchen sink and toilet thrown at us."

I have known Dick and Joanne for years. I was blessed to counsel with him when his business began and blessed more to watch it grow into a major building supply firm. He made some interesting observations during our conversation. He said, "You know, we have to remember that all our money belongs to God and we have to treat it as such. We must be good stewards of what we get." Then he went on to give examples of well meaning Christians who get into trouble in business by using poor judgment, and as he said, "By the time they get to me, their boat is twenty miles off shore with a hole in it and their radio is out." Dick said again, "It is His money."

On a more personal level, our church (Word of Life Family Church) in Burlington grew from about 100 people to about 500 within the past three years. They needed a place to grow. I was privileged enough to be the Campaign Chairman to help pull that small group together and purchase a building and 8.6 acres at a prime location. It looked impossible at the time, but our church has over 83% of its people who tithe. Less than three years later, we are housed in a building worth over $3,200,000 and we are eating away steadily at paying the mortgage off.

Time after time I watched those who pledged go through unexpected hardships. In my own case, within six months of Mary and I making a sizeable pledge, we had a business deal cost us five times that much. *But we kept giving and today we are seeing God restore it and more.* In fact, we met that pledge by following the leading of the Holy Spirit for three years.

The bottom line here is we need to do what Dick Hudson said we must do. Let me ask you some questions.

If we believe the money we control is God's money, does it make sense for us to spend it quicker than it comes in?

If we believe it is His money, do we jeopardize the safety of our employees by not setting aside enough money to insure the business can operate without owing everybody in the County?

If we believe it is His money, do we place our family in danger by signing notes we stand a fair chance of not being able to pay off?

If we believe it is His money, do we drive fancy automobiles and live in the richest community if we can't pay our creditors?

If we believe it is His money, do we jeopardize our testimony by entering agreements that are not prayed through and thought through?

If we believe it is His money, do we dare to tell "white lies" in order to get more money?

If we believe it is His money, do we cheat our clients or customers when we get the chance?

Having said all that, the question is, if we believe it is His money, what should we do?

We should understand that when times are good, we should set aside what we can (after tithing and giving alms) to see us through that unexpected bump in the road.

We should use everything we possess to its fullest extent rather than buy the most recent technological toy that makes us feel good.

We should save enough money to weather through any financial storm for our family and/or employees.

We should be careful about paying more for products or things than they are actually worth.

We should expect our clients or customers pay us timely while we strive to give them the best service. Do not hesitate to collect your accounts receivable early as possible and pay your accounts payable as late as possible without hurting your credit or relationships with your creditors.

We should accumulate enough to see our family financially secure if anything happens to us.

We should accumulate enough to see our business survive if we were temporarily out of commission for a few months.

We should accumulate enough to be able to buy bargains when others get into trouble. Like it or not, a downturn in the economy can be a jewel for someone who has money on hand to take advantage of it.

I could give you example after example of Christians who see money as an evil. In fact, I believe some church-goers think it is righteous to be poor and have very little money. I remember the first time I made this statement to a church audience, "Christ is King in the Kingdom of God, but Cash is King of Business." I could immediately tell those who worked in businesses and those who had a less realistic view of how money works in this world. In fact, some of the dear saints looked embarrassed when I said it. But, it is the truth!

Did you ever ask yourself why Jesus had a treasurer? I believe it was because they needed money to pay for the traveling ministry plus give to the poor. Remember when Judas Iscariot left the table at the last supper, some of the disciples thought he had gone out to make contributions to the poor?

Look at all the parables and examples Jesus gave about managing money. He used money to illustrate forgiveness, to illustrate the using of what God gave us, to illustrate giving to God, to illustrate how to run a business. He even admonished us to estimate a cost before we obligate ourselves to a project. Jesus knows today as He knew then what role money plays in the world.

One of His best illustrations is in Matthew Chapter 25. I like the Living Bible translation because it is very easy to understand. Jesus was explaining how the Kingdom of Heaven was like a man going into another country and gathered together some of his employees and loaned them some money for them to put to work while he was out of town. It reads like this:

He gave $5,000 to one, $2,000 to another and $1,000 to the last-dividing it in proportion to their abilities, and then left for his trip. The man who received the $5,000 began immediately to buy and sell with it and soon earned another $5,000. The man with the $2,000 went right to work, too, and earned another $2,000.

But the man who received the $1,000 dug a hole in the ground and hid the money for safekeeping.

After a long time their master returned from his trip and called *them to him to account for his money. The man to whom he had entrusted the $5,000 brought him $10,000. The master praised him for his good work. "You have been faithful in handling this small amount," he told him, "So now I will give you many more responsibilities Begin the joyous tasks I have assigned to you."*

Next came the man who had received the $2,000 with the report. "Sir, you gave me $2,000 to use and I have doubled it." "Good work" his master said, "You are a good and faithful servant. You have been faithful over this small amount, so now I will give you much more."

Then the man with the $1,000 came and said, "Sir, I knew you were a hard man and I was afraid you would rob me of what I earned, so I hid your money in the earth and here it is!"

But his master replied, "Wicked man! Lazy slave! Since you knew I would demand your profit, you should have at least have put my money into the bank so I could have some interest. Take the money from this man and give it to the man with the $10,000. For the man who uses well what he is given shall be given more and he shall have abundance. But from the man who is unfaithful, even what little responsibility he has shall be taken from him. And throw the useless servant into outer darkness: there shall be weeping and gnashing of teeth."

I do not believe Jesus would have used the illustration about money unless He knew the exact role money plays in this world. Look at what He said. The guy who doubled his $2,000 was told that he was faithful and now he was going to get much more. The guy who doubled his $5,000 not only was told he would have "many more responsibilities, but to begin the joyous tasks being assigned to him." Then he got the original $1,000 the lazy guy had to begin with.

Believe me, the Bible talks so much about money and how to handle it, we would have to be dumb and blind not to see the role it plays. The bottom line is, if God can't trust us with money, how can he trust us with much of anything else?

That of course, includes getting into debt instead of working to get out of it. We have been sold such a bill of goods in today's society about staying in debt to get a "good credit score" we have lost all sense of what debt is. We should beware of borrowing more than we can pay back or on terms we can't meet, which leads to my next chapter.

WHAT IS CHAPTER SIX ABOUT?

1. A prudent businessperson with cash will tithe 10% to his church. How much should he/she pay to themselves above their weekly needs? _____

2. Explain why you think prosperity will ruin a fool.

_____

_____

_____

3. Do you *really* think a Christian person in business faces challenges with money that an unbeliever does not face? Yes _____ No _____ Why?

_____

4. What could prompt a businessperson to live in a big house, drive a fancy car and owe creditors he/she could not possibly ever pay?

_____

5. Is it against your Christian principles to take advantage of a situation where others fail and you have the money to buy them out? Yes_____ No _____Why?_____

6. Do you *really* know how to look at the money in your account as God's money instead of yours?
Yes _____ No _____ Why?

_____

7. Though we may have money in the bank, is it prudent or scriptural to get the best bargain we can when we buy something? Yes ____No _____ Why?

_____

8. Explain in your own words why you think cash is king in the business world. _____

_____

_____.

9. Do you think money is the root of all evil? Yes
_____No _____Why? _____

_____

10. Do you think God will judge us by how we use the money and resources He gives to us?
Yes _____ No _____ Why?

_____

7 The Borrower is Servant to the Lender

The rich rules over the poor and the borrower is servant to the lender. [Proverbs 22:7 NKJV]

Did you ever stop to think how lending institutions make their money? One simple explanation is they lend the same dollar many times to several borrowers with interest. Did you ever stop to think that when you borrow $100,000 on a mortgage over a thirty year period at 6.5% you pay back $277,544.49? The bank didn't give you gold, they didn't give you cash, *they just gave you a piece of paper!* Not only that, but when you make your payments, they use that paper to lend to somebody else, and on and on it goes. They didn't risk very much if their lending officer is smart, because he had an appraiser certify to him that your property was worth more than you borrowed. They are betting that you and others like you will keep paying and if you don't they will take the collateral back from you and re-sell it again. Though banks incur loses, they keep them small enough in order to preserve their bottom line.

We live in a society that is conditioned to debt. Our kids in high school aren't even taught how to balance a checkbook and if they go to college, they are inundated with credit cards.

Why do you think that is the case? Because the credit card lenders are banking on ole' Dad and Mom bailing the kids out of debt! Recently on TV, a college student was asked why she ran up over $15,000 in credit card debt. She said she hadn't been taught how interest works. *And she had made it to college!* What had her parents taught her? What had the social scientist teacher taught her except a lot of junk about being politically correct and cultural diversity? Enough already about diversity and political correctness! How about teaching our kids how to add, subtract and balance a checkbook, for crying out loud.

Heaven knows our politicians haven't learned about debt, because they continue to spend over the budget. Why? *Because it isn't their money they are spending, it is yours.* Our governments and our people are knee deep in debt. We are more concerned over our credit score than the amount we owe. What a sick outlook on monetary matters. When someone asks us how much our automobile costs us, we say $700.00 per month instead of the cost of the car and the cost of all the payments and insurance plus tags and taxes. We are like a group of ostriches with our head in the sand.

Although we sit idle and watch our children expect instant food, instant gratification and instant religion, we never tell them there is always a debt to pay if we instantly borrow money. That law works the same for adults.

Zig Zigler once said there are three things impossible to do. (1) Kiss a girl leaning away from you. (2) Climb a fence leaning toward you and (3) Borrow yourself out of debt.

No truer words were ever spoken. Yet, we seem conditioned to see something we want or think we need for ourselves or our business and think, "How much can I borrow?" **Be very careful of debt.** It will kill you or make you wish you were dead. Use it if you have to but know what happens if you can't meet its obligations.

A dear friend of mine was a very successful home builder. He was an astute businessman and was a committed Christian. He built a shopping center in a good location and had it about 90% leased. He had good anchor tenants and several out parcels left up front on the main road to sell. His shopping center was appraised at about $12,000,000. He had worked, sweated, put his own money into the venture and had borrowed $4,200,000. He had done everything right. The money he owed was from a bank that based its construction loan on a permanent mortgage lender financing the center, and the mortgage lender had given him a commitment to take out his construction lender. The only problem he had was, a recession hit and his permanent mortgage lender found itself over-committed, so they failed to fund his permanent loan. His construction lender licked its chops when that happened because they saw their construction loan period coming due. They demanded the $4.2 million construction loan to be paid rather than extend his loan, or they would foreclose on his shopping center.

My friend didn't have that much cash, so there he sat. Troubled was not the word. He was mad and he told me one day, "Those so and so's were trying to steal his twelve million dollar shopping center for four million dollars." I looked at him as straight in the eye as I could and said, "My friend, you don't have a twelve million dollar shopping center, what you have is a four million dollar debt." He blinked his eyes and said, "You know, you are right." So, he spent several weeks holding off that debt until he got enough investors to buy his out parcels so he could pay off the construction loan. He lost a lot of money by having to give up the "gravy" on the entire piece of real estate because he did not have enough cash to bail himself out. Of course, he could have lost the entire shopping center, including all his cash he had spent on it.

Banks should post a sign outside that says, "To err is human, to forgive is not bank policy." Maybe some of us would get the message.

Over the years, I have noticed that things don't change much. When the economy is good and cash is flush, the banks are forced to find ways to lend money. Have you ever noticed how friendly your banker becomes during those periods? If you happen to own or run a business that is doing well, you get visits; get free lunches and every courtesy from your banker. When you need a loan they are ready willing and able. *They can't do enough for you, it seems.*

However, if things begin to get tight, you become a liability to your banker. If you become delinquent on your loan, suddenly he is pressured by his peers to make sound judgments on how to deal with you. You must realize that bankers are promoted if they don't have losses. A banker who has several delinquent accounts might as well find something else to do for a living. So, there are no more free lunches and very few courtesies. The conversations all turn to how you are going to get the bank out without loss.

If I might say so, over the years I have found bankers are like everyone else. Some of them are more self-confident than others. If you have a banker who is frightened of his position and you are in trouble with cash flow, look for some swift harsh action. I have dealt with some who did the best they could under the circumstances. Those I will always cherish are those who stood by me and helped me walk through the hard times. I must warn you that one of the reasons they stood by me was *the minute I realized I was in trouble; I carried them to lunch and told them of my predicament.* Many times, things would work out without their help, but as long as I kept them abreast of the facts and they felt comfortable with me, they would give me the space I needed to work things out.

After having said all this about bankers, it is best to operate without loans as much as possible. Now, I'm not saying you shouldn't borrow money for your business. I'm saying when you borrow, know your need, and know how much you will need. *I will pause here to say that one of the worst mistakes is to borrow about 75% of what you need. One day, you find yourself obligated to a loan too small that didn't help you generate enough cash flow to pay it back properly.* It is a tough sale to go back and raise the loan amount, but it can be done with enough preparation. Most of all, *know how you are going to pay it back and monitor that progress rather than just "hope you can make the payments."*

Business Credit Cards

Now a word about using credit cards in business. The credit card advertisers try to sell a business owner on the ease of keeping record of expenses. In fact, some cards are advertised as being strictly for business owners. What they don't tell you is how it works *in the real world.* Most of the time in order for credit cards to be issued to a business (especially small and medium sized) the owner must sign a personal guarantee for the credit cards that will be given to the employees. So, if you have five people with credit cards traveling and using them for lodging, meals, gas, and whatever, it is logical that you can expect $15,000-$20,000 per month on those cards. Even though you get the holder (your employee) of the card to guarantee the limit amount, good luck on trying to get him to pay it off if the two of you have a disagreement. Especially, if the employee/cardholder has done something a little dishonest or beyond his authority, guess who will pay the price? Not him/her. Besides that, he feels like he incurred the expense *because of you.*

The invoices for card payment are issued once per month, so when you get the bills on say, the 8th of any month, those credit cards usually cover a period of expenditures that are already old. They are old enough that you can't do much about them but pay them. For example, if you get your bill on July

8th for the month of June the card charges can run from May 25th until June 25th. By the time they go through your accounting department, say by July 20th, you are about ready to be billed again. If someone in your accounting department sees small charges that look illegitimate, they will usually march them on through because they have so much work to do. There is no telling what some disgruntled or spaced out employee could have done by that time. I have known business owners to wake up to a mountain of credit card debt created by their own employees. The credit card companies couldn't care less until you approach against the limit on any of the cards because they are getting about three times the interest than what they could loan the money based on collateral. After all, they have the personal signatures of the company owners.

Never allow credit card payments to go past the 30 day period. Pay them off first because they have a higher rate of interest than any other vendor you deal with.

I worked as a consultant for an owner of a large business who decided he was taking matters in his own hands. He had over fifty people who were on the road in his vehicles and spending money for gas, fuel, parts, and materials. His weekly expenditures averaged from $25,000 to $30,000 per week. He refused to give anyone a credit card. When I asked him why, he was quick to tell me he had been there and done that. He said some employees would stop for gas and add their lunch on the bill. He said credit cards caused him to lose control over his expenditures and besides, he didn't want to wait until he had $120,000-$130,000 in credit card bills hitting him once per month.

At first, I thought his method was a little bit wild, but the more I watched the philosophy behind it and how it worked, it was ingenious. He operated a large construction company spread over two states. He looked at each individuals' needs, whether a Project Manager, a Superintendent or Foreman. He also looked at how far they operated from his main office and based on those factors, he would decide how much cash to give each of them. For example, a Project Manager might be given $5,000, a Superintendent $2500 or a Foreman $1,000. That was for *weekly expenses.* When I asked him if it wasn't a little risky to write some foreman he didn't know well a check for $1,000 in advance, his reply was, "No, I know that the $1,000 is as much as he can steal from me and besides, I have his weekly paycheck "in the hole." So, his risk wasn't that bad and he was paying *no interest* on any of it. It was very simple, when each supervisor sent his weekly report, including pay-roll report; he included *weekly paid receipts* for every dollar he had spent. When his payroll check went out via overnight de-livery on the following Thursday, he was reimbursed.

That system made a lot of sense for several reasons. First, it kept everyone on a short leash and accountable. If they didn't turn in paid receipts once per week, they would run out of company funds and have to ask for help. When they asked for help, they were held accountable.

Secondly, it made the paid receipts visible every week. One person in his office went through every expense report every week and approved or disapproved expenditures that were *less than a week old!* He didn't hire an extra clerk to track it. His receptionist did the approvals between phone calls. Of course his receptionist was given authority to approve, disapprove or ask questions. That same receptionist also wrote the expense checks from an expense account, and was held accountable if a spot check later turned up anything that looked fishy on the receipts.

This business owner or his son signed every check written; he delegated no authority to anyone else to do that. (That is not a bad idea.) Once the checks were written, it took only about three hours per week for one of the accounting people to record those expenses spent the previous week, *and show what each person with an expense account had spent each week (in separate columns) for the past four weeks.* At a glance, the owner could look down the list and see who his big spenders were for the week and the last month. Once again, if anything looked wrong, a more detailed accounting could be done.

Thirdly, the remark the business owner made about keeping control of what his employee could steal from him should not be written off. Understand that some employees will steal from you every chance they get. I realize for every ten good employees who wouldn't misappropriate one dollar there is probably one or two who is either sloppy or dishonest. It's always easy for politicians and slothful employees to spend your money. Whatever your system, try to get the information as soon as possible and control it the best you can considering the business you are in.

We see movies about the mean old banker foreclosing on the family farm, or the widow's house or in a few instances, a competitor buying out his business rival's mortgage. In all those scenes, we see the wailing and gnashing of teeth by those caught up in the web of debt. I can tell you from personal experience there are times when things change so drastically you can't help but get caught up in a web of debt, but when you do, here are some points to remember.

- As soon as possible, conduct a spreadsheet showing what you owe and when it is due.
- Get a plan in place after looking at your cash flow from the normal business you perform daily or if you can create cash from the sale of assets. (Be conservative in your spreadsheet about what you can sell, when you can sell it and how much you can bring in by the sales as well as cash flow from your business weekly.)
- As soon as you have a plan, call your lender and get him/her on board. It would be wise to suggest to them

what the likelihood is if they try to move quickly or foreclose. Most smart bankers know that if they do anything to curtail or shut off your cash flow, they are less likely to ever get paid.

· When looking at your short term or long term debts, arrange payments so those things you personally guaranteed get paid off first. Remember, if all else fails, you don't want to face personal judgments and/or sheriff collections. (Don't panic early on about this because from the time a threat by a vendor is made to the filing of a complaint and hearing of a matter you have a lot of time to work things out. Do your best to keep anything from going to the status of a judgment.) Most creditors know that an even a judgment is no good without means of collection, so when it comes down to it, most will work with you.

· Your first order of business is to look after your family the best you can. That means if you are faced with a week where you have $5,000 to pay on a $50,000 debt, set aside $1,000 for your family and spread out the $4,000 the best you can. If it all falls, see your family is fed first. That is according to Scripture you know because one who doesn't look after his own family is worse than an unbeliever (I Timothy 5:8).

· Be honest with everyone. Don't make promises you can't deliver and when you make promises based on someone's promise to you, don't think twice about what to do if their promise fails. (It all runs downhill doesn't it?) *Call whoever you promised and tell him the truth and keep him posted as things change and get better and/or worse.*

It has always been a good idea for me to put my priorities in order and paste them on my bathroom mirror. They help keep me focused. Things like who to pay first, who to pay second, third or fourth should always be kept in your mind. That works for big priorities, like (1) Work to pay off current equipment, (2) Work to pay off mortgage on office/warehouse (3) Work a reducing all debts to banks based on accounts receivable. (4) Begin to accumulate cash in a money market account. Usually, the last priority is growing your own wealth, but that shouldn't be ignored, especially when things begin to turn for the better. Pray and trust God to show you how to juggle what and when to let something drop. I know that sounds a little pious when you're in the middle of a mess, but it is the truth.

Finally, don't beat yourself up because you got yourself into a servant situation with your lender. Learn from it, take a good look at what circumstances got you there and move on. That leads to my next chapter. It is worthwhile reading.

WHAT IS CHAPTER SEVEN ALL ABOUT?

1. A lending institution makes it money by
_____the same dollar many times to several
_____ and they didn't give you gold or
cash but a piece of _____.

2. In your opinion, why do our high schools spend so much
time on teaching political correctness, environmental issues
and diversity instead of practical things like balancing a
checkbook?

_____

3. If you have a property appraised at $12,000,000 and owe
$ 4,200,000 should you see it as equity of $7,800,000 or as a
debt that must be paid of $4,200,000?

_____.

4. If you are borrowing money for your business, which is
worse? Getting a commitment from the bank for more than
you need or getting a commitment for less than you will
need? _____

5. If you have several people on the road incurring expenses
on your companies' behalf, is it wisdom to issue them company credit cards or allow them to use their own and you
reimburse them for their expenses?

_____

6. If you get in trouble with huge debt owed to banks, who
should you contact first? Your pastor ____
Your spouse _____ Your friends _____ Your banker
_____.

7. If you find yourself working out of a deep debt owed to several different entities, prioritize these actions according to your own beliefs. Pay those screaming the loudest _____ Ask God for wisdom and follow His leading _____ See your family is covered monthly _____ Worry about your reputation _____ Continue to tithe _____ (Itemize 1-5)

8. Do you think a Christian has extra pressure in paying their debts because they don't want to hurt the cause of Christ or discourage unbelievers? Yes _____ No _____.

9. Are we as a society, failing to tell our children the downside of creating debt? Yes ___ No ____.

10. If we acknowledge God helped us gain our assets (money, property, things), should we be very careful about borrowing against them? Yes ____ No ____ Why _____

8 | What About this "Guilt Thing?"

There is therefore now no condemnation to them which are in Christ Jesus, who walk not after the flesh, but after the Spirit. For the law of the Spirit of life in Christ Jesus hath made me free from the law of sin and death. [Romans 8:1-2 KJV]

This chapter will be the shortest chapter in this book. Not because the subject matter isn't important, but because we should give very little space to guilt in our Christian life.

Whether talking to psychiatrists, counselors, pastors, and teachers, or by observing situations most of us know first hand there can be no doubt that guilt is one of the most damaging deterrents to human life. Guilt wrecks marriages, homes, businesses, relationships, good judgment, health, and certainly the mind. As always, different belief systems say different things about guilt. Most secularist say there should be no guilt because it serves no purpose but to hamper those who have it. That is elongated into "do what you want and forget about it." The problem with that approach is the effect it has on others and the lack of learning on the part of the one who incurred the guilt in the first place.

On the other hand, there is the approach by some religions that "guilt and shame must be paid for by suffering, shame and pain." *Well, I have news for both extremes.* Christ has already paid for the suffering, shame and pain, and *if you belong to Christ,* you can experience the freedom from it, *if you re-pent.* That doesn't mean you might not have to pay on earth for some things you did wrong, but it doesn't mean God is holding you in low esteem either.

I have seen successful businessmen who worked their entire lives to build a financial empire only to realize they missed building a lasting family. Their wives either hated them or tolerated them. Their children either didn't care to be around them or stayed just long enough to get what they wanted. Guilt drove them to drink, find other sexual interests that produced further guilt. That eventually led to losing their business. In some of cases I believe the inner core of guilt they were carrying caused them to find ways subconsciously to destroy what they had built. Let's face it, guilt says, "You don't deserve to be a winner because...."

There is a big difference between *condemnation* and *conviction.* There is no doubt a Christian will be convicted if he goes off the reservation and does something stupid. For example, if a pastor woke up with a hangover in a whorehouse, there is no question about him having a *strong conviction* from the Holy Spirit. In fact, he would well know he had done wrong before anybody else found out about it. He could be truly sorry; he could repent and actually go through every step of forgiveness of his sins. In I John 1:9 we are reminded that *"If we confess our sins, he is faithful and just to forgive us our sins and to cleanse us from all unrighteousness."* The spirit of the pastor I mentioned could accept this truth, his wife might even accept it, but if his soul *(his mind, will and emotions)* never accept it, he will wallow deep in the condemnation that follows. Condemnation can paralyze you and can place you squarely in the middle of a losing life forever on this earth. It can ruin your relationships; your business and your will to excel at anything.

I know my illustration about a pastor in a house of ill repute is a little strong, but condemnation doesn't allow for a degree of sin. It can take root from a lot of little failures. It can set in your mind because of who you are trying to be versus who you really *think you* are. It can stop you because your parents, your wife, or a teacher might have helped you form a mindset about things that you just aren't capable of doing. Let's face it, if you don't have a desire or conviction to do something, you are working against your calling. On the other hand, if you begin something and see it failing, you have to see it through until the end. That can test the best when it comes to guilt and condemnation. Condemnation is nothing but prolonged guilt. When guilt has been accepted by an individual condemnation will finally do them in.

Guilt comes in all sizes and packages. If you have decided you are smart, guilt can set in because of pride. First Timothy 3:6 says if a Christian leader must be seasoned. It says he better not be a novice, *"lest being lifted up with pride, he fall into the condemnation of the devil."(*KJV) If you think you are dumb, condemnation can set in on you and tell you there is no use trying. *This business just isn't for you. You were born in the wrong time, the wrong community, your parents were poor, and you really have no right to be trying to be successful. Besides that, who do you think you are anyway, trying to rise above your peers?*

Take a good look at the meaning of the two words. Condemnation in Greek is the word *"Krima"*. It means *"the effect of a crime, to punish, to sentence."* We can also view the word condemnation as it commonly refers to the state of a building. When a building is condemned, it is declared "unfit for use or unsuitable for habitation." Guilt will make you feel unworthy every minute of every day. Conviction in Greek is *"elegcho", meaning to confute, to admonish, convince, tell a fault, rebuke or reprove.*

Certainly, a person with a conscience directed by the Holy Spirit will be convicted. He will be admonished, convinced he did wrong, he will be rebuked, BUT thank God he can make a quality decision, which is to ask God to forgive him and *believe that He has!* The whole message of Christ dying for our sins would be a joke if we couldn't do that with a clear conscience. Yet, religious tradition keeps us in guilt or condemnation, clearly going against the message of the Gospel.

From personal experience, I have never experienced condemnation for doing anything crooked, dishonest, or particularly sinful. Guilt just has a way of building up *with little failures.* I have always known a parent should provide for their children not vice versa, and once when I had to use up the savings accounts of my two youngest children to meet payroll, it took me years to forgive myself. Truth was, they got over it and couldn't have cared less, and I was able to not only pay them back, but made a down payment on a home for each of them later when they grew older. That guilt or condemnation I carried for years wasn't worth a pinch of dehydrated owl manure. It was there until I began to realize that Jesus died for me to take that guilt upon Himself, and if I didn't believe that, I should forget the whole Christian thing and live like a heathen.

In fact, I have come to realize it is a sin to allow guilt and condemnation to bother you. The instructions are clear. In 2 Corinthians 10:4-5, we are told that not only do we have the ability (weapons) to get rid of guilt and condemnation, but it tells us *how* to do it.

For the weapons of our warfare are not carnal, but mighty in God for pulling down strongholds; casting down arguments and every high thing that exalts itself against the knowledge of God, bringing every thought into captivity to the obedience of Christ. (NKJV)

What does this mean? It means that God has given you and I the ability and power to use our weapons of faith, of hope and our mouth to cast down every argument, and anything else that even appears to go against the knowledge or word of God (and He knows things will always work out if we hold on to our faith). It is our job to capture our thoughts and bring them into captivity. You've got it—capture those sucker thoughts one at a time. When those thoughts come up in your mind, cast them down. Talk to them *out loud*, start looking at something else, and get off that thought! Use the name of Jesus; He will help you do it. It will be tough at first, but every day it will get easier. Start talking positive and speaking positive scriptures. It changes your mind, your faith, and it will eventually change your circumstances.

I have known men and women who have accomplished so much in their lives and when they come to a big bump in their road, they become completely defeated. I have seen businessmen who "just gave up" when their business went bankrupt. It cost them their health, their wife, and their hope. Yet, I have seen others walk through bankruptcy and before you know it, they are back with a new business, a new outlook and a new smile. What is the difference?

One allowed condemnation and guilt to be his undoing. The other used his conviction as a stepping stone to use his faith and just kept on truckin.' Both people were good people with two different approaches to trouble.

Remember, there is no such thing as being defeated, *if you refuse to quit*. Use every defeat to learn what you missed. Sometimes it was because you were a little naïve; sometimes it was because you miscalculated; and sometimes it was because you were too trusting of people and didn't hold them accountable. Sometimes it wasn't anyone's fault because the market changed and you could not respond in time; and finally, sometimes we find ourselves in the wrong place at the wrong time.

One of the worst things for a Christian to deal with is how to handle creditors who are screaming at him. Especially, if his business is in a free fall and failure is imminent. Here is a word of advice: Take a look at why you went into business. You did it to make a profit and to improve your standard of living, and so did each of your creditors. You knew it was a risk, and if they didn't, they were blind or stupid. Try to do the best you can, talk to each of them, and if it is impossible to treat each one equal, do the best you can and then forget it. If your conscience dictates that you come back in another venture and pay them, then do it. Having coached many businesses through turn-a-rounds, there is one thing for certain: if the owner breaks his back to get everyone paid, though it was later than expected, there will be those creditors who really appreciate what he did. However, there will be others who will never forgive him for being late.

I remember when I owned a construction company that experienced $860,000 damage in one night due to Hurricane Camille, I struggled for about eighteen months to get everyone paid. There was a credit manager of a big equipment account that I promised to pay in full. The bill was about $93,000.00. I wiggled, twisted, finished, collected, sold, and finally paid everyone off. I thought he would be tickled beyond measure I had kept my word. That joker almost ruined my credit because he was mad that I didn't pay him the interest. I finally told him one day, "Hey, you are fortunate that I stuck with the misery for a year and a half just to get you paid."

Memories like that can give you nightmares. It can make you wonder what is wrong with you, dummy. It can promote guilt that you aren't living up to what you and everyone else expected, or it can bring fear strong enough that you will never risk again. Don't do it. It isn't worth it.

Remember that each day you get up, your spirit is renewed and circumstances will change for the better if you continue to work toward that change. Never give guilt a place in your life.

Finally, remember the scripture I gave at the beginning of this chapter? It says if we are in Christ we are free from the law of sin and death. What is the "law of sin?" What is the "law of death?" In fact, what does "the law" mean in that verse?

The word used for law in the Greek there is *"momos." It means to parcel out, it is law through the idea of prescription usage or a genitive (possessive) case.* It is something that is used in certain cases. Here it is the law that frees us from sin and death. What is sin? Sin, in the Greek simply means *missing the mark (so as not to share in its prize), to err. It comes from the word "hamartano."* We all know what death means, it just means to die or be dead, period.

How many times do we all miss the mark in our lives spiritually, mentally, physically, financially and socially? Ask forgiveness, get up and forget about it. God has, because he said He has.

- If guilt is plaguing you, get on your knees, ask God to forgive you of failing, then get up and know He did. Get over it! (I John 3:19-22)

- Study positive scriptures and speak them to your own soul and spirit every day, things like "Satan has no power over me because I overcome evil with good." (Romans 12:21)

- Or other confessions like, "He who knew no sin became sin for me so I could become the righteousness of God." (2 Corinthians 5:21)

Do not give guilt one small toehold in your life. It cannot stand against the Word of God and a strong will from you.

WHAT IS CHAPTER EIGHT ABOUT?

1. Does guilt or condemnation have a place in a Christian's life? Yes _____ No _____ Why

_____

2. What is the difference between guilt and condemnation?

_____

_____

_____

3. How do you get rid of guilt?

_____

_____

4. If condemnation doesn't come from the Holy Spirit, where does it come from? _____
 If the Holy Spirit doesn't condemn what does He do?

_____

5. In your opinion, is it a sin (falling short of the mark) to allow guilt or condemnation to control your life? Yes _____
No _____ Why _____

6. If you are in Christ, the only way for you to have defeat is to _____.

7. If guilt is plaguing you, ask forgiveness, then get up and know He did. Get _____ !

8. In your opinion, is "feeling sorry for yourself" a part of guilt or is it driven by selfishness. _____

_____

9. In your opinion, what does confessing solid scriptures over your situation do for you? _____

_____

10. Do you think our holding on to guilt hampers the work of God in our lives? Yes _____ No _____

9 Four Reasons Christians Fail Financially

Wisdom shouts in the streets for a hearing. She calls out to the crowds along Main Street, and to the judges in their courts and to everyone in all the land. "You simpletons!" she cries, "How long will you go on being fools? How long will you scoff at wisdom and fight the facts?" [Proverbs 1:20-22 TLB]

■ While living in Chesapeake, Virginia, I was suddenly awakened at four in the morning by what seemed like a still, small voice inside my spirit and mind. "Get up," the voice said, "I have something to tell you." "Can't it wait until morning?" I whispered, not wanting to wake Mary.

The voice continued, very nice, but very forceful, it said, "Get up. I am going to give you four major reasons Christians fail in business." I thought to myself, well, it can't take too long to write down four things, so I stumbled up, found a pad and pen by my bed and dragged into the bathroom, turned on the light while sitting upon the "throne" (with the lid down). As my head began to clear, I became excited. I thought, "Wow, this is going to be quite a revelation." In fact, I felt a little guilty because I had been so slow to respond. Then, I heard this and wrote it down. I will never forget the impact of those words. The voice said:

"Son, the number one reason Christians fail is *they don't use Godly wisdom.*

They don't constantly walk in faith.

They don't understand the law of giving.

Finally, He said, *"They don't constantly walk in love."*

I pondered His words for weeks. Then I began to study the Word and revelation came that made so much sense to me. It took a while to figure it out, but I came to understand there could be several reasons for a business to fail, but what I had received were *spiritual reasons that Christians fail financially.*

Let's face it, if I were to ask an unbeliever if he thought Christians have a harder battle in business than unbelievers, he would probably say, "You Christians are nothing but a whining bunch of pansies who complain about everything. You don't have it any harder than anybody else."

If I asked an atheist if he thought Christians have it harder in business, he would say, "That's stupid. There is no God. There is no devil. There are only dollars and cents and your ability to adjust. Successful business is for the guy who has the most guts and who can take advantage of any situation quickly. It's about being smart and taking advantage of the other fellow."

If I asked most Christians in business do they think they have a harder time conducting business than unbelievers, the following are what I would probably hear. (As a matter of fact, I have heard them.)

"Are you kidding? The more I try to profit and give into the Kingdom, the more opposition I encounter. Do you know, being in business for myself has really made me aware of the kingdom of darkness and how it fights anything in the Kingdom of Light."

"I can't explain it, everything was set up to succeed by good business practices and things began to happen out of the blue that cost me a fortune."

"The more I try to do the right thing, it seems the more I have opportunity to do the wrong thing."

"It is hard to explain, but I have seen what seems like one giant hand closed my cash flow for no apparent reason."

One Christian entrepreneur said, "I have come to understand that when I am depending on a big sale, or a big loan, or when I have a big item to pay off, it seems like whatever I depend on to happen suddenly is interrupted or stopped with a series of unbelievable chain of events." "Things come out of the woodwork for no other purpose than to stop what I am doing." Bottom line, I have never met a seasoned Christian businessperson who doesn't believe that God has angels to work for us and Satan has demons who work against us.

For those skeptics who call this foolish, may I quote what Paul wrote when he began to tell us how to win every spiritual battle in Ephesians 6. It seems he believed he should tell us who or what we were fighting. He put it this way. "For we are not fighting against people made of flesh and blood, but against persons without bodies—the evil rulers of the unseen world, those mighty satanic beings and great evil princes of darkness who rule this world, and against huge numbers of wicked spirits in the spirit world." (Ephesians 6:12 TLB) Thank God, Paul then instructed us how to win the battle with them every time.

One thing is for sure. If we are battling with spiritual beings that can influence the minds and hearts of those people we deal with daily, as well as attack our minds with depression and fear it begs the question. How do we fight them *spiritually? That is where the battlefield is—in the spirit realm.* We've been taught for years that whatever occurs in the spirit realm will manifest itself in the physical realm. I love what the Bible tells us to do in that circumstance. It's simple. As Ephesians 6:13 says, we are to "take up the whole armor of God, that we may be able to withstand in the evil day *and having done all to stand...Stand... (Or keep on standing).*

Now, no one can stand unless they know why they are standing. If you don't know what you are standing upon to defeat the devil's every move in your life, then you had better find another line of work. If he realizes you are quick to give up, he'll give you many chances to do so. He CANNOT defeat you as long as you are a doer of the Word, and not a hearer only (the same as His Will) and do not give up. Remember, the Word will work in your life if you let it! James told us how to allow our humility to God to cure our worldliness. In James 4:10, he said it as plain as anyone can say it. "Therefore, submit to God. Resist the devil and <u>he will flee</u> from you. Draw near to God and He will draw near to you." That is a promise. God cannot lie.

Let's take a look at the four spiritual reasons Christians fail in the financial and/or the business realm.

Reason # 1: "They don't use Godly Wisdom."

What is Godly Wisdom? Where do you get it? How do you practice it?

<u>What is Godly Wisdom?</u>

Godly Wisdom is revealed throughout the Bible. In fact, it is mentioned 234 times. He must have been serious about our getting His meaning. Before we go any further, let's agree on a few things that are indisputable. God is many things and one of the things He is, is Wisdom. After all, He created the universe. He created the earth and made it inhabitable. He cre-

143

ated man and woman. He created all animals, all materials. There is nothing created that He did not create. That took Wisdom. It took imagination, physics, mathematics, and more than we can imagine. Most of all it took faith.

God is the ultimate manufacturer. I used to own a Cessna 421 twin engine plane. Although I trusted the flying of it to an experienced pilot, I soon learned that he constantly referred to the owner's manual. He was good at his trade, but he knew that if he didn't continue to study *what the manufacturer recommended, he might forget something and stick that airplane into the ground like a dart!* I was glad he did, especially when we encountered bad weather. He not only memorized that manual, he would constantly refer to it. Well, our manufacturer knows how we are made, because He made us! Our formula for everyday success and victory is to *constantly refer to our Manual.*

What does the Bible say about Wisdom? Obviously, we could fill pages upon pages, but here are some known facts from our manual about Wisdom. I hope you can find what Wisdom is, and even if I fail telling you, keep looking into His Manual until you are satisfied that you know what it is!

In the Old Testament, the Hebrew word most commonly translated for wisdom is the word "chokmah." It means to have wisdom in a good sense. To be skillfull, to have wisdom; act wisely, to have good wit. It comes from the Hebrew root word, "chakam," which means to be wise in mind, word or act. We would probably call that *good instinct or common sense* in today's vernacular.

In the New Testament, the Greek word used to describe wisdom is "sophia." It simply means higher or lower, worldly or spiritual wisdom. It comes from the root word "sophos" and that means to be wise in a general application. So, certainly Godly Wisdom means to be wise in mind, word or act in the spiritual and worldly realms. We can gain all kinds of spiritual wisdom and still not know how to act wise in worldly affairs. However, the opposite is equally true. What we see in the business world most of the time is people using worldly wisdom and knowing absolutely nothing about spiritual wisdom. God has both types of wisdom and we need both in order to operate in this world. Jesus said we were "not of this world," but if you notice, He left us in the world to operate our affairs. We had better learn how to deal with it.

Take a look at what the disciples figured out when trying to organize a way to keep their community of believers going in the right direction after a spat between factions. They knew what to do, because the twelve brought the parties together quickly and said this. "Therefore, brethren, seek out from among you seven men of good reputation, *full of the Holy Spirit and wisdom, whom we may appoint over this business."* (Acts 6:4) They were looking for seven guys who had both spiritual and worldly wisdom or good common sense in both realms.

Psalm 111:10 gives us a clue on how to get a "leg up" on worldly wisdom. The psalmist writes, *"The fear of the Lord is the beginning of wisdom. A good understanding have all those who do His commandments."* If we don't begin by yielding to the reverential knowledge that God and His Word are the ultimate source of all wisdom, we might as well forget about getting His Wisdom. It is a choice, like anything else. We can't get wisdom in either the spiritual or worldly realm without knowledge, and the beginning of wisdom is to acknowledge that God's way of thinking, acting and doing things are superior to worldly wisdom. Once we have made that choice, it is a matter of *gaining the facts and acting on them in faith.*

I know some of you are saying, "Well, what if I try and miss it?" Don't worry, His grace is sufficient to help us get up, dust ourselves off and go at it again. However, when you dust yourself off, go back to the Word and understand why you missed it. Look at II Timothy 3:16, Romans 15:4, 1 Corinthians 10:11, and Psalm 119 and remember that God's word is the source of all wisdom. Those scriptures certainly tell us that the "school of hard knocks" and mistakes are not God's best method of instructing us.

Where do we get Godly Wisdom?

The Bible is so full of wisdom; it is hard to miss it. Look at a few of the following scriptures. Jesus wasn't just making conversation when He said "Seek and you shall find" or "knock and it shall be opened." *If you don't seek after wisdom, you will not find it, period!* It is not something you are *going to try; it is a way of life.* I personally don't think we can ever find it all, but we can surely find more than our schools, colleges and plain old hard knocks can give us. (Although, school, college and experience will help as long as we look at their teachings through the lens of what the scriptures teach us.)

Look at Proverbs 3:13-26: (NKJV) Who wouldn't want to find this kind of wisdom?

> *Happy is the man who finds wisdom,*
> *And the man who gains understanding:*
> *For her proceeds are better than profits of silver*
> *And her gain than fine gold.*
> *She is more precious than rubies,*
> *And all the things you may desire cannot compare with her.*
> *Length of days is in her right hand,*
> *In her left hand riches and honor.*
> *Her ways are ways of pleasantness,*
> *And all her paths are peace.*
> *She is a tree of life to those who take hold of her,*
> *And happy are all who retain her.*
>
> *The Lord by wisdom founded the earth;*
> *By understanding He established the heavens;*
> *By His knowledge the depths were broken up,*

And clouds drop down the dew.

My son, let them not depart from our eyes—
Keep sound wisdom and discretion;
So they will be life to your soul
And grace to your neck
Then you will walk safely in your way,
And your foot will not stumble.
When you lie down, you will not be afraid;
Yes, you will lie down and your sleep will be sweet.
Do not be afraid of sudden terror,
Nor of trouble from the wicked when it comes;
For the Lord will be your confidence,
And keep your foot from being caught.

Notice we are not promised that once we find wisdom, all our problems will go away and will never return. That would be a false promise. As long as we are in this world we will encounter problems. The bigger we dream and the more we accomplish, the bigger the problems become. If we find Godly Wisdom, we can win over those problems every time, that is, if we don't give up and trust in the Lord. I once read that "getting old ain't for sissies." Well, running a Christian business in a secular world "ain't for spiritual sissies either." It is a matter of having trust in the Lord inside of you. When we miss it, we just go back to the Manufacturer's Manual.

Did you know that we believers are commanded to get wisdom? Look at Proverbs 4: 7-9 (NKJV). I don't think He is making a suggestion that *maybe* we should get wisdom.

Wisdom is the principal thing
<u>Therefore get wisdom</u>
And in all your <u>getting, get understanding</u>.
Exalt her, and she will promote you

147

She will bring you honor, when you embrace her
She will place on your head an ornament of grace;
A crown of glory she will deliver to you.

The Manual says that wisdom is the *principal thing.* That means the *first thing, the chief thing.* In fact, He then commands us to get it. But He is quick to point out that wisdom isn't worth so much if we don't get understanding with it. The Hebrew word for understanding used there is "biynah". It means to get the *perfect meaning.* Personally, I believe that includes:

> How it works
> Why it works
> When it will work as well as...
> What keeps it from working
> Why it will not work
> When it will not work.

The Word of God is full of examples of those answers. Of course, practical experience also will teach us, but who wants to stumble through a thousand mistakes to find ten types of understanding to get wisdom? It takes study, prayer and experience. You may say, who has the time? My answer is an old construction adage. "Why did we never have time to build it right the first time, but always find the time to tear it down and rebuild it right." We have a lifetime to learn understanding and to get wisdom. If we go into eternity only getting forty things right pertaining to wisdom, we are better off than going to heaven learning how to recover from one hundred and forty mistakes. I know, because I have made a bunch of them. How much time do we use up on this earth overcoming mistakes when we could be patient and learn wisdom and understanding before we make them? Certainly, we would have more time to devote to God's destiny in our lives, not counting all the heartaches to ourselves, our employees and our family.

Did you know that our Manufacturer's Manual tells us the difference between Heavenly Wisdom and Demonic Wisdom? Take a look at James 4:14-18 (NKJV). I love reading Proverbs and James for I call them the two "business books" of the Bible. Solomon and James had a way of telling it like it is!

Who is wise and understanding among you? Let him show by good conduct that his works are done in the meekness of wisdom. But if you have bitter envy and self-seeking in your hearts, do not boast and lie against the truth. This wisdom does not descend from above, but is earthly, sensual, demonic. For where envy and self-seeking exist, confusion and every evil thing are there. But the wisdom that is from above is first pure, then peaceable, gentle, willing to yield, full of mercy and good fruits, without partiality and without hypocrisy. Now the fruit of righteousness is sown in peace by those who make peace.

How do we apply this teaching to things in the business world on a daily basis? How can we not be a little "self seeking" when we are looking after the interest of our company or ourselves? I would say the first place to look and see if we have any envy or pride in our hearts against our competition or the person on the other side of any deal we are making. Envy won't work. Pride won't work. Praying for favor and looking to God to help us get better at what we are doing will work. Asking for forgiveness for envy or pride will work. Asking the Holy Spirit to guide us on the right path will surely work. We already know that where envy, strife, or pride exists it will only bring confusion and every evil thing to the surface. We should look at ourselves and our organization carefully and when we find envy and strife or pride we should attack it and kill it like a rattlesnake in our kitchen. Don't let it live.

At the same time, we should judge our motives. I believe God is much more interested in our true heart motives than he is in our making a few dollars. To use wisdom that is pure means wisdom that is chaste, clean, innocent and pure. That does not mean we shouldn't have wit about us or walk into a stupid deal that will hurt us now or in the future. It is a pure thing to want to make an honest profit and *do things that are honest and have integrity.* It means we don't lie, cheat or steal, but it does not mean we give up the farm and all that goes with it to someone who will. To have wisdom that is peaceable, gentle, willing to yield, and full of mercy means we don't squeeze the very last dime out of a deal just because we can take full advantage of the person we are dealing with. On the other hand, it doesn't mean we give up more than we can afford because we want to be a "nice Christian." *Godly Wisdom is something we need help from the Holy Spirit to understand.* Most of all, wisdom that is without partiality and hypocrisy is wisdom that does not give in to things that you know are wrong, dishonest or illegal just to make things work or get a deal closed.

How many times have we all allowed ourselves to agree to something that looked good on the surface only to find that it wasn't what we thought it was because it didn't pass the "smell test?" How many times have we done it because we did not want to offend someone we admired or thought was a better businessperson than we are? That is showing partiality and is certainly hypocritical. Godly Wisdom will stay away from those types of deals, regardless of how good they look on the surface.

I have found a law at work among Christians. If you think I am kidding, look at the religious leaders who have fallen due to something they knew deep inside was wrong. Look at the politicians who hold themselves out to be Christians only to be toppled from power and end up in disgrace. Peter was exactly right when he said, "For the time has come for judgment *to begin at the house of God,* and if *it begins with us first,* what will be the end of those who do not obey the gospel of God." (Peter 4:17 NKJV) That law is *if we hold ourselves out to be*

<u>*Christians and try to hide illicit, illegal or immoral acts, we might*</u> <u>*as well know we are going to be the first exposed.*</u> If we go into situations knowing they are crooked, look not only for them to fail, but also that we will be exposed. If you have done those things and you aren't bothered by them, ask yourself this question. Have I gone beyond hearing from God? Is my conscious seared? Pray for forgiveness and work like the dickens to get yourself out of the mess, regardless of cost. He will forgive you and help you find a way out. Be prepared to face the consequences.

Did you know there is hope for all of us in obtaining wisdom? Proverbs 8:5 says, "Oh, you simple (someone seducible and foolish) understand prudence and you fools, be of an understanding heart." As long as we *have a heart toward understanding* we can study The Word and gain the knowledge and wisdom. If God had decided you were too foolish to obtain wisdom, He would have never commanded you to get it in the first place. That should be consolation to all of us.

Did you know the Manual has provisions to assure us we can get Godly Wisdom? All you have to do is study, ask and believe in faith. James made it as simple as one possibly could. I like James. I believe he had a business type mind. He was short and to the point. Either you get what he says or you just don't want to get it. Knowing he was raised up in the same household as Jesus, he had some keen insight on Wisdom. *Hey, James was a guy who was reared in a household with Wisdom.* Surely, it must have been a transition for James to grow up wondering what kind of weirdo his older brother was and siding with the family who thought Jesus was out of His mind when he began His ministry. Once though, he saw his older brother stone cold graveyard dead on that cross, buried in a tomb and then have that same brother suddenly show up and have a one-on-one conversation with him prior to meeting with the other guys, (I Corinthians 15:7 *"After that He was seen by*

James, then by all the apostles) James became a true believer. There is no wonder he opened his epistle with these words, *James a bondservant of God <u>and of the Lord Jesus Christ.</u>* James recognized the teachings of his older brother were true. He and Jude had up close studies of an older brother they finally recognized as being the Son of the Living God in an earthly body. They knew He was Wisdom.

James tells us how to get wisdom in his "take it or leave it" manner. Read it carefully and if you don't have Godly Wisdom, here is how you get it. He was so sure that he had the nerve to tell us that we would profit from our trials. In fact, he seriously implies that we *gain Godly Wisdom* from our trials.

My brethren, count it all joy when you fall into various trials, knowing that the testing of your faith produces patience. But let patience have its perfect work, that you may be perfect and complete, lacking nothing. If any of you lacks wisdom, let him ask of God, who gives to all liberally and without reproach, <u>and it will be given to him. But, let him ask in faith, with no doubting, for he who doubts is like a wave of the sea driven and tossed by the wind. For let not that man suppose that he will receive anything from the Lord; he is a double-minded man, unstable in all his ways.</u> [James 1:2-7 NKJV]

The first time I read that James said we should "count it all joy" when we got into a mess I thought, "God, You must be kidding." The more I studied and prayed, the more I could see that the only way to count something as "all joy" is if you defeat the trial. That made sense when I saw that it had to be His timing and not ours. That is where the patience comes into play. But *look at what he says.* He says if we stand in faith with patience, we will win every time. How could you not win every time and become perfect and complete, wanting nothing, unless one of two things happened.

1. Either you have complete victory over the trial and get the desired results.

2. Or you see God has used it to open a better door for you during the trial.

Anyone caught in various trials knows he/she needs Godly Wisdom to get out of the mess or to turn it around for good. In fact, it takes Godly Wisdom to have victory over every trial or have it turn out for the best. It is as if James' next thought was, "I guess you are wondering how to be perfect and complete, wanting nothing, well here it is. Ask for Godly wisdom and guess what? If you will do it in faith, nothing wavering or doubting you will get Godly wisdom."

Once I was in the middle of so many trials it looked like a trial snowstorm. One thing after another began to collapse, from the economy to my bank account, to my company and to my employees. I went to read James and said, "Lord, I am asking you for wisdom. Your kind of wisdom. I receive it by faith and I know I have it. Thank you Lord. Amen." Over the years it has worked every time. When days turned into weeks, and weeks into months, barely keeping my head above water, I stood, knowing if I "wavered" I could expect nothing. How many of you reading this knows there cannot be a "testimony" without a "test." One morning, I screamed out to God and asked him what did "wavering" mean. This is what I heard in my spirit and I wrote it down. "*Wavering is wondering when I am going to do it and how I am going to do it.*" "Oh Lord,' I said, "That is hard medicine." Since I got no further answers I figured that was all I was going to get. He was right. The breakthrough came through in His timing when He had things lined up. Not only did it give God a view of my faith, but it built my faith tremendously. I learned to look to God as my source and not some person, bank or economy. That was the greatest gift of wisdom He gave me through that ordeal.

So, James has a clear message on how to gain Godly Wisdom. The steps seem simple, but the faith level is built and the reward comes with the wisdom He gives you. Here are some things I received out of the Book of James.

1. If you are in fiery trials, laugh at them the best you can knowing that if you are a born-again Christian, and do not cast away your faith and patience, you will win, sooner or later. If you stand in faith, you can't lose. <u>The only way to lose is to quit.</u>

2. As you walk through the trials, as often as you need it, ask God for wisdom and thank Him for giving it to you liberally. (Remember, He will give you only what you can handle at the time, so be sure you practice what He gives you, by faith.)

3. Don't doubt and don't waver. Take the Word of God that pertains to your situation and each time doubt creeps in, confess those scriptures out loud. Fear and doubt will subside and finally leave. Focus on love that casts out fear.

4. Don't be double-minded. Once you believe God had told you something, go for it and if it doesn't seem like it is working from the get-go, know it is up to Him to direct you. He won't fail you.

5. Finally, don't dread every day. Thank Him. Praise Him whether you feel like it or not. He will honor that.

Now we come to the most interesting part.

<u>How do we practice Godly Wisdom?</u>

I know we have brushed on this subject during the two prior questions, because one can't talk about what Godly Wisdom is and where to find it without bringing in some illustrations on how to use it. I believe the first thing we have to decide is this.

Do I really believe God loves me and wants to see me succeed as His child? If you are a parent, you already know the answer. The trouble is most of us have no problem believing God loves *somebody else* and will intervene in *their lives, but we don't know so much about ourselves.* Why do you think that problem exists?

Well, for one reason, many of us were raised in environments where we began to see God as an old white bearded guy with a sword and hammer, and he was ready to pounce on us like a chicken on a Junebug. How many parents have told their children or have at least implied, "God will get you for that," or 'if you do that God won't like it." Of course He doesn't like sin or unbelief, but He has surely seen a bunch of it over the years and He still put up with it. Why? Because He loves us and doesn't want to see one of us spend eternity in hell or live on this planet in defeat.

Being a father helped me understand God's love for me. I look at all seven of our children. Each of them has various talents and abilities, different personalities, different levels of faith, different levels of perception, different levels of common sense. They have different ideas on success, and they have different desires, day to day.

Do I love each of them equally? Yes!

Do I want each of them to obtain their idea of success? Yes!

Do I recognize each of them are "wired" differently? Yes!

Do I want them to learn from their mistakes? Yes!

Do I think they all have different abilities and talents? Yes!

Do I want each of them to prosper and be in health? Yes!

Though I may identify with the thoughts and ideas of some of them more than others, will I still treat each of them according to their needs? Yes!

Who gave the ability to me to "act" that way? God did, because I didn't have a clue about being a parent. I was an only child. I know that is true because I see it over and over in His Word. *That is how He acts toward us. He is "no respecter of persons."*

155

What could possibly make you think that God loves everybody else but you? That doesn't make good sense. It goes against His Personality.

Once you have decided that God loves you, you can begin to look for His Wisdom and how He wants to convey it to His children. We can identify it in His Word through prayer and study. The question is, how do we put it in practice?

The first mention of wisdom in the Bible is Exodus 28: 3. God wanted to teach the Israelites how to make consecrated garments for Aaron in order for him to properly worship Him, so He filled them with the Spirit of Wisdom. In those days, people didn't have ready access to the Holy Spirit like a believer has today. Jesus Christ gave us access to the Holy Spirit. *The average Christian doesn't realize what a Gift that is.* Notice the first thing God gave the Spirit of Wisdom to people was for them to practice a craft that ultimately allowed them to be skillful at their vocation. That ought to tell us something.

God also placed a Spirit of Wisdom into craftsmen for them to build His temple. (I have always thought it took a lot of wisdom to build things.) Exodus 36:5 says *Then Moses called Bezalel and Aholiab, and every gifted artisan in whose heart the Lord had put wisdom, everyone whose heart was stirred, to come and do the work. And they received from Moses all the offering which the children of Israel had brought for the work of the service of making the sanctuary. So they continued bringing to him freewill offerings every morning. Then all the craftsmen who were doing all the work of the sanctuary came, each from the work he was doing and they spoke to Moses, saying, "The people bring much more than enough for the service of the work which the Lord commanded us to do."* (NKJV)

Where God places the Spirit of Wisdom, there is always more than enough to do the job. All we have to do is ask for it and believe we have it!

I believe one of the first steps in practicing wisdom is to

<u>talk wisdom</u>. *Watch your mouth because your ears are listening!* What you see, and especially what you say is what you will believe. Take a page from the Psalms. Psalm 37:30 says, *The righteous speaks wisdom and his tongue talks of justice. The law of God is in his heart. None of his steps shall slide.*

Psalm 49:3 says, *Hear this all peoples. Give ear, all inhabitants of the world. Both high and low, rich and poor together. My mouth will speak wisdom and the mediation of my heart shall give understanding.*

You simply can't practice wisdom unless you begin talking like it, studying like it, thinking like it and eventually you will act like it. It helps to start dressing like it and acting like it from the beginning. That builds faith. *When you have gone through those steps, you will begin practicing wisdom.* Building wisdom and knowledge is like anything else, first the seed, then the blade and then the ear. Be patient and you will know when to harvest. That goes for whatever you do in your personal life and business life.

One way to practice Godly Wisdom is to simply use the advice given in Proverbs. Take a look at some of that advice.

Proverbs 4:27 (NKJV) says *Ponder the path of your feet and let all your ways be established. Do not turn to the right or the left; Remove your foot from evil.* The Hebrew word translated into the word "evil" means natural or moral adversity, afflictions, calamity and grief. So practice pondering where you are going and look at the results before they happen. Once you know that don't turn to the left or right. Stay focused.

Proverbs 6:5 (TLB) says, *Son, if you endorse a note for someone you hardly know, guaranteeing his debt, you are in serious trouble. You may have trapped yourself by your agreement. Quick! Get out of it if you possibly can! Swallow your pride; don't let embarrassment stand in the way. Go and beg to have your name erased. Don't put it off. Do it now. Don't rest until you do. If you can get out of this trap you have saved yourself like a deer that escapes from a hunter or a bird from the net.*

So practice keeping your name off of notes that include people that you suspect will react in their own interest if the note becomes due. Don't do it! *You will get burned most of the time.*

He who tills his land will be satisfied with bread, But he who follows frivolity is devoid of understanding. (Proverbs 12:11 NKJV)

Be careful that you stay focused. Do not follow worthless pursuits or pies in the sky. There is no guaranteed easy way to succeed in business. Practice staying on track and measure your success often. If some deal sounds too good to be true, it usually is.

Commit your thoughts to the Lord and your thoughts will be established. (Proverbs 16:3 NKJV) This passage is definitely something we should practice.

The Hebrew word for commit means to "roll, seek, trust and wallow" your thoughts to the Lord. This is a promise that He will guide you to establish the correct course of action. *This will only work if you talk to Him about your thoughts and plans of action before you embark on them.* Practice doing that and then waiting for His answer. Many Christians make the mistake of dreaming up a deal, signing up for it and then ask God to bless it. Sometimes, that is a little late in the game.

Those scriptures of advice are only a few. Get into Proverbs yourself and find out what applies to your situation. Get into the entire Bible and *practice what it tells you.* You will find yourself making Godly decisions using His Wisdom.

Reason # 2 "They don't constantly walk in faith."

There is so much to say about faith. In fact, thousands of books have been written about faith. It seems to me that faith is the bedrock of all that we believe to be holy, steadfast and unchangeable. If we, as Christians were to believe only two scriptures in the Bible, for me it would be John 10:10 and Hebrews 11:6. Jesus plainly tells us that the thief (the devil) comes only to kill, steal and destroy and that Jesus came that we might have life more abundantly (John 10:10). That is the dividing line in the Bible. This puts the question to us, "Who are we going to follow?" Well, the obvious answer is we follow Jesus. The 11th Chapter of Hebrews is all about faith, but verse 6 nails it. This verse is very clear to me. It simply says it is impossible to please God without faith and that those who come to Him must believe that He not only exists, but that He rewards those who diligently seek Him.

These two scriptures also tell me that if we want any kind of abundant life, we must operate in faith. I noticed that that little voice in my spirit that morning said we must *constantly* walk in faith. The word constant means to stand firm, to be consistent, or exhibit consistency of mind. The definition of faith in the Greek is "pistis" and it means a persuasion, credence, a moral conviction of religious truth or the truthfulness of God. Simply put, we *must never take a vacation from our faith. We must never lose it or ignore it. It is the key to pleasing God and having any kind of abundant life. It is the key to victory and success in this life and beyond.*

When we accept Christ as our Savior, Romans 12:3 (KJV) tells us that God has dealt to everyone *the measure of faith*. I'm glad it didn't say a measure of faith because many of us would go around complaining that He gave some of us more faith than others. No, everyone is given the same measure of faith, but it is like anything else. *Faith must be exercised if it is to grow stronger.*

Faith is a Law and is just as sure as gravity. When it is linked up with patience, it will grow. We must never forget though, that it will only work when connected to love. Paul wrote that faith works by love. In other words, we can't pray for God to hurt someone and have faith that He will. We can't send a $10,000 check to pay a bill when we only have $200 in the bank. That's not faith—that's breaking the law and stupid. The results will be a stay in jail or a fine and embarrassment for writing a bad check.

I believe there are five things we ought to know about how faith works. I am sure as you practice yours, you will learn even more.

1. <u>Faith won't work in an unforgiving heart.</u> Read and study Mark 11:22-26 and Ephesians 4:26-32.
2. <u>Faith is a spiritual force, not a mind or head force.</u> In fact, if you try to understand faith with your head, all you will get is a headache. Read and study II Corinthians 5:5-9 and Romans 8:6-14.
3. <u>Faith must be released with words from the heart.</u> We can't believe one thing and say another. Read and study Jude 1:14-20 and James 3:1-10.
4. <u>Faith works whether you feel like it is or not.</u> It works both in the positive as well as the negative. Look at Joseph in the Old Testament, he was a good example of one who at times did not feel like it was working, but he stayed with his faith in God. Read and study Luke 8:41-56.
5. <u>Faith comes by hearing (and hearing and hearing and studying) the Word of God.</u> You can hear it preached, taught by persons, by tapes, by DVDs or by reading it out loud to yourself Read and study Romans 10:12-17.

I also believe there are four short things to remember about faith, if it is to work in our lives. This idea is not original because most people who practice faith already do it on a daily basis.

1. Say what the Word says.
2. Do what the Word says.
3. Receive what the Word says.
4. Tell what the Word has done for you.

So, how does that work in business? What do we do when it looks hopeless? Permit me to use another personal circumstance to explain.

By 2004, Mary and I had experienced many reasons to exercise our faith. I was 72 years old and she was 61. We believed that God had directed us to buy certain assets from a failing company and that we should keep its good young people working. So, we borrowed against our own home and land that was debt free and invested about $500,000 into the venture. We invested in a contracting business that performed overhead and underground construction services for clients such as Time Warner, Comcast, the out-of-bankruptcy company Adelphia (who had to pay its bills timely by law) and Viasys.

That was in 2003, and the first year looked marvelous. We had a good profit and the future looked good. Cash flow was fairly well, that is, until we realized that due to the dot.com failure, a lot of the "big boys" were re-organizing and cutting their budgets. Still, we believed that if we stood strong, we would be one of the few survivors in the industry and would have even less competition. As the cash flow began to dry up, we began to finance our accounts receivables, but things still looked OK. The reason they began to dry up was because the big boys were slow in paying. Finally, the big boys stopped paying old bills; hoping businesses like ours would give up and fade away. We decided to close the business.

In June of 2004, our church began a building program because it needed more space for its congregation. It was already having a Saturday night service and two services on Sunday. It needed to purchase the entire building of which it

leased about 25% of the space. It also had to expand its parking area. The church had begun with about 37 members and
had grown to over 300 at the time. I was asked to be the Chairman of a "Giving to Grow" campaign, and all of us were asked
to pray for a commitment to give whatever God told us to give
over the next three years. Mary and I prayed for weeks, and
agreed that God was giving us the same number. When we
both asked each other what we were hearing, both of us were
afraid to tell the other for awhile. That number was $100,000!
We looked at our assets, our company, and did what we believed God told us to do. So, we committed by August, 2004.
It was decided that those in the congregation who could, would
give 10% of their commitment as a first payment because the
church had to place a large down payment and finance the
balance of purchase and construction. The big day for everyone to give their first payment was the end of September, 2004.

Meanwhile in August of that year, we attended a convention for Communications Contractors and saw that we were
about the only surviving company our size still in the business. We both knew that things were not going to be as rosy as
we had thought, and came back from that convention knowing we had to downsize the company. About two weeks later,
we learned that our Controller, who filled out the reports to
the bank for borrowing against our accounts payables, had
overstated our receivables and that instead of showing a profit,
we suddenly learned that the company was $600,000 worse
off than we thought. Our books suddenly showed a loss. I
blamed myself, but the complicated way of billing for that
business contained so many different invoices (there could be
over 300 invoices for one month) and most of the mistakes
and overstatements were in "works in progress" or work complete but not yet billed. That was a third of our business an-
nually! We had changed Controllers about six months earlier
and the new guy went back for months to reconcile billings.

Talk about sick at the stomach. I reviewed his new findings about four o'clock one Friday afternoon in early September, 2004. I prayed hard over the weekend and felt like kicking my own behind. That weekend, I called my old friend Anthony Aliamo, and he flew in on his own time and that Monday we surveyed everything to be sure of the numbers. We made an analysis and constructed a cash flow chart forecasting how we were going to close down the business while getting the banks paid.

My first step was to call my banker and tell him what I had found. Anthony went with me to meet him and lay out the bad news. The banker knew me and told his superiors that I was a man of integrity and would see it through. Not only had we signed personal notes to whatever the company owed the bank, but we had signed another note for a short term $500,000 loan. At the time we owed about $1,800,000 that we were personally responsible for. We were devastated. We also had made a commitment to our church based on prayer.

The worse part over the next several months was making decisions that would seriously affect the outcome. Downsizing, finishing up projects while collecting back billings became a priority. When my pastor Rich Fennelle found out, he came to my office and asked what he could do. I will never forget him saying, "I guess you are searching for some answers aren't you?" I said, "Rich, I don't even know the questions yet."

I knew the next Sunday was the day that I had committed to give my first $10,000 on our pledge. I also knew that the bank would be calling on us to pay any of our personal money in their bank toward the current deficit.

God and I had a little talk. I remember telling Him that I had always said I would know whether He was in the deal or not by how the company prospered. Yet, I knew He was in this deal, no matter how bad things looked, for He had promised to never leave us or forsake us. So, to affirm that, I told

Mary to immediately write a check for $10,000 and give it to "Giving to Grow" as our first payment on the $100,000 commitment. About two weeks later, after the bank had taken all our savings, I received an unexpected $1,000, so I decided to give it to the church just to show God, the devil and everyone else where my priorities were. Then I thought, all I had to focus on was our commitment to come up with another $22,333 within the next twelve months. (At $33,333 per year pledged for three years).

I believed that it was up to me to practice what I had preached about faith. If I was going down, I was going down practicing my faith and the rest was up to Him. So, over the next few months I came up with priorities and posted them on my bathroom mirror so I could see them every day as I shaved. Within twenty-four months, and by fighting and collecting from the "big boys" plus refinancing our house mortgage we paid the $1,100,000 owed to the bank. These were the priorities posted on my mirror.

1. Pay Word of Life Church commitment.
2. Pay off mortgages on our home.
3. Pay off the $500,000 debt above the bank loan
4. Build up personal wealth.

Within three years, we paid the church commitment, had reduced the mortgages down to $240,000 and the other debt down to $400,000. Our personal wealth wasn't what it once was, but we never missed a payment, a tithe or a meal. Bear in mind, the commitment was over and above the tithe. Sure, there were times when we thought our commitment was big, but we both believed we served a big God.

The hard part was to decide how to distribute any dollars that came in. I decided to not let guilt set in, but to first look after my family and then follow my priorities. I depended on the Holy

Spirit to guide me. He led me to a wonderful consulting job to provide a good living for us while cleaning up the other mess. I had to make some hard choices. I had to allow some people to get very angry at times, but I believe we followed God's directions the best we could. Some companies were compromised and some companies did not get paid. That's business.

Needless to say, the world's advice was to declare bankruptcy and start over. I believed God's Word was true. I believe today that the best is yet to come

So, serve God, do the best you can and don't quit. Faith without works is dead. You will come out a winner.

Reason # 3 "They don't understand the law of giving."

If we are serious about learning the law of giving, we have to take a look at God Himself. He is a Giver. The Creator of this universe and all matter and mankind is a Giver. Here are just a few examples of things that quickly come to mind.

- He gave His only begotten Son, who died for us, and then the two of them sent His Spirit in his Son's place to guide us. That's giving at its best!

- He is a giver of life. He breathes life. Acts 17:28 says He has given us the awesome right to be *in Him*. He sent His own Spirit to inhabit our spirit. *"For in Him we live, and move, and have our being, as certain also of your own poets have said, for we are his children."* That is certainly giving us more rights than a Buddha, or Mohammed or any other false god. *Think about it!*

- He gives us healing. The Bible is full of examples and promises. We have all seen them first hand, if we have been looking.

- He gives us increase. The law of planting and reaping is shown to be His system throughout the Scriptures. Read I Corinthians 3: 6-15 as an example.

- He gives us victory in every situation. If you don't think so, just read I John 5: 3-5.

- He gives us Wisdom. (We have already explored that idea).

- He gives us richly ALL things to enjoy. I Timothy 6: 17 says so.

- He gives us ability. I Peter 4: 11 explains it.

- He gives us the power to get wealth. Read Deuteronomy 8:18

Of course, He puts some rules and regulations in place in order to keep us from misusing His Giving Power, but He is an established Giver.

If we are to be an imitator of God, and we are made in His image, it is clear that we should be givers also. In fact, Jesus Himself put it this way. "Give and it will be given you, good measure, pressed down, shaken together, and running over will be put into your bosom. For with the same measure that you use, it will be measured back to you." (Luke 6:38 NKJV)

It is obvious that the law of seedtime and harvest is applicable in everyone's life, whether they are Christian or non-Christian. Most thinking people really believe "you reap what you sow" or "what goes around comes around." But how does this apply in the business realm?

- If we give good service to our customers or clients we

will <u>receive</u> good will, more business and should increase our profits.

· If we <u>give</u> good pay, good working conditions and encouragement to our employees we will <u>receive</u> more production, more loyalty, and more people who will take responsibility within the company and should increase our profits.

· If we <u>give</u> attention to detail in our operations, our accounting and our reputations, we will <u>receive</u> more knowledge, wisdom and will enjoy the image of efficiency and integrity. Certainly, that will lead to a solid profitable organization.

· If we <u>give</u> to our church, the poor, and to those we know need a helping hand, we will <u>receive</u> blessings from the Lord many times over what we give. Those blessings can come as good health, peace of mind, long life as well as financial blessings.

There is no doubt if we give, we must learn to receive. I had a hard time with that part of God's cycle for a long time. The Scriptures are full of examples of people who did not have sense enough to receive what God was trying to get to them. I think the secret to learning how to receive is learning to be grateful. Once we realize how much we have been given, it is easier to see those things we should receive with gratitude. It seems once we begin looking for things to thank God for, the more they continue to roll in to us.

So, I believe the "Law of Giving" has three basic parts.

1. Giving to God. (Tithes and Offerings)
2. Giving to the Poor. (Helping families one on one or through an organization)
3. Giving to Others. (Let's talk about that one a little)

Giving to others can be a tricky thing in business. If we give *too much* to employees or customers they come to expect more than we can afford. Or in the case of employees, they may become complacent thinking they've got it made.

I truly believe we will always come out ahead if we obey the principle found in Ephesians 6:9. In that passage we are told to be eager to give our very best to our boss. In fact, we are to serve him as if we were serving Christ. We are admonished to work hard when the boss isn't looking as well as when he is. We are promised that the Lord will reward us for each good thing we do, whether we are the employer or employee.

Then in verse 9, the boss is given a pretty stern message and that is to treat the employees right just like they were told to treat him. The boss is commanded not to keep threatening his employees because both the boss and the employee have the same Big Boss in heaven.

So, how are we to act when we are in the middle of hard negotiations over a deal? Are we to give away the farm? Of course not! We are to use wisdom, but don't lie, cheat or steal. Does that mean telling *everything bad* we know about the deal for the person on the opposite side of the negotiation? No, that is being stupid, but it is wrong to cover over a lie, or have something hidden in the deal that you know will hurt the other person once the deal is done.

For example, it would not be right for you to portray a tractor-trailer as being in excellent shape when you knew the transmission was shot, and you had packed it with grease to keep it from grinding. That is dishonest. On the other hand, if you told the prospective buyer that the transmission was bad and you had it packed it with grease, but everything else was in good shape as far as you know, and let him know he was buying it at his own risk, that is fine.

Finally, giving is a day to day thing that a Christian should monitor in his heart in everything he does and should ask the

Holy Spirit to guide him correctly, hour by hour. He will. I know that if we *take rather than give* in our relationships, our lives, our businesses, and with God, we will never prosper in *every area of our life.* That means spiritually, mentally, physically, financially and socially.

Reason # 4: "They don't constantly walk in love"

This is a tough one for a believer. It is impossible for an unbeliever. As a businessman or as a consultant, it seems like everything is about confronting adversarial situations. It is appropriate that this subject be the last one to study. ***This principal is absolutely the most difficult subject to understand and to practice day by day in the world of business.***

A semi-retired businessman approached me after I gave a brief synopsis of "the four reasons for failure" in our church one Sunday morning. He said, "This is a tough one. I call it threading the eye of a needle." He is correct, but I believe it is a matter of the heart. All of us, whether we are Christian or not, have that constant battle between what Paul so aptly described as "between the spirit and the flesh." I know all of us who believe in Christian principles battle between what we know we should do and what we seem compelled to do according to business practices. After all, not only is business confrontational, it is always competitive. If we have thrived in the world's system, it is a learning experience to walk in love while being hard nosed. It can be done though, because that is exactly how God deals with us.

The Scriptures on one hand command us to always show concern for others before ourselves but they also admonish us to never be slack in business. At times, that seems to be a dichotomy. *I believe it is a matter of always listening to the Holy Spirit in every circumstance and following His lead.* I didn't say it was easy; it *is the necessary and right thing to do.* He knows what the right thing to do means in every circumstance.

In order to keep our head and hearts in tune, it is important to realize that God Himself is Love, and if He is in us, then we have the ability to practice the same kind of love. Years ago, it helped me to understand when I read what true love looks like based on I Corinthians 13:4-8. It is especially clear in the Amplified Version. Here is a confession I use often. I just reasoned that if we are to be an imitator of God, then we have to do what He does. If He is love, then so are we. This is how I confess it out loud so I can hear me say it.

"Because God's love is in me, I endure long and I am patient and kind. I am never envious nor boil over with jealousy. I am not boastful or vainglorious. I do not display myself haughtily.

"I am not conceited or arrogant or inflated with pride. I am not rude or unmannerly and I do not act unbecomingly.

"I do not insist on my own rights or my own way. I am not touchy or fretful or resentful. I take no account of an evil done to me and I pay no attention to a suffered wrong.

"I do not rejoice at injustice and unrighteousness, but I do rejoice when right and truth prevail.

"I bear up under anything and everything that comes. I am ever ready to believe the best of every person. My hopes are fadeless under all circumstances and I endure everything without weakening.

"Because I have God's love in me I never fail and I never fade out or become obsolete or come to and end.

"As long as I constantly walk in love, I cannot fail."

The part about "not insisting on our own rights, not being touchy or resentful and never taking into account an evil done to us or paying no attention to a suffered wrong" can be tricky if we forget one basic principal thing. *Never take things personal during negotiations, or when confronting people or situa-*

tions. Continue to do what you think is the right thing for your company and the individual or circumstances you are confronting. By the time I get to the end of that confession, I already know in my heart what the answer to my problem is. It is then a matter of getting off my backside and doing it.

I will never forget an estimator I hired for a construction company's branch office. He said all the right things, and he really wanted to do the right things, but he just didn't have a clue about being an estimator. What made things worse, he gave me a little card carrier with the inscription in gold saying, "I can do all things through Christ which strengtheneth me. Philippians 4:13." I still had it my pocket, full of business cards the morning I fired him. I tried to explain how he just did not know the basics of estimating costs and he didn't want to hear it. It was uncomfortable, but I knew *for the betterment of the company and for those who depended on his estimates being real when bidding multi-million dollar projects,* I had to let him go. I don't know his heart, but I believe he felt like I did a very un-Christian thing in firing him. I never took it personal and I prayed for his future in the business. I hope he did the same. I would recommend him as a good person to a competitor, but I would not recommend him as an estimator. I loved him and fired him in the most gentle way I could. That's all that God asks of us.

I believe love in action for a believer is to serve God, serve our family and our fellow man. I also recommend that same order of priorities. I used to look at the same Holy Spirit working in Mother Teresa as well as Pat Robertson. Mother Teresa became an icon of love and faith, though the news media recently has tried to make a lot of noise about one letter she wrote while fighting for her faith. On the other hand, the name Pat Robertson has become almost profanity to the media, who seems to dwell on everything he says that does not line up with their ideology.

While both of them have their followers, who has done the most for God, their family and mankind? Even though Mother Teresa gave her life loving and treating children in Calcutta's poorest district she was able to help only a few. Pat Robertson, through his Operation Blessing programs has given food, medicine and hope to millions around the world. Do I think both of them practiced the God kind of love? Yes. Do I think Pat Robertson helped many more worldwide than Mother Teresa? Yes. Do I think each of them served where God placed them? Yes.

That is the key. As people in business, each of us must serve God, our families and our fellow man *in the arena we are called to serve.*

Once again, we need to make a big improvement in *being careful with our words.* In Ephesians 4:29-31, we are commanded to be aware that we can grieve the Holy Spirit by what we say. Believe me; we can grieve those who hear our words on a daily basis.

Today, through the media, books and the general decline in civility, we are bombarded by words once thought of as too coarse for public use, or too abrasive, or just blasphemy. The surprising thing is they are used openly without restriction. Not only do they grieve the Holy Spirit, they should also grieve us. They are so engrained in the business world, we all get caught up in them. We should never use profanity when talking to a group or when in anger. I confess that is one of the biggest strongholds I have had to overcome. I also believe it is the cause of some of the biggest misunderstandings I have become involved in.

So, what kind of language grieves the Holy Spirit and shows us that we're not walking in love?

1. Certainly, cursing does and we should never, ever use God's name in vain.

2. Speaking against the Word, like praying for something and then saying it isn't coming to pass.

3. Speaking ill of someone or carrying gossip from one person to another.

Why do they grieve the Holy Spirit, you might ask? Here are a few reasons.

- It stops God's angels from working on your behalf.
- It wrecks your faith.
- It opens the door to Satan.
- It doesn't please God.
- It hampers those who look up to you as a Christian.

Faith works by love and faith without works is dead. How can we have faith when we are not walking in love? If we find ourselves not walking in love or saying things that grieve the Holy Spirit, we need to repent. Then we should forgive the person who triggered the incident and praise God. He inhabits our praise, you know. When we make that connection back to Him, He gives us the cover to carry on.

I know the business world is a dog-eat-dog world. That's how it will be until the millennium. The world's financial system will eventually fail because it was set up by a failure himself. His name is Lucifer or Satan. If you think I'm kidding, look at the worldly system. It is *based on fear and greed*. Yet, though a believer is not to conform to this world, the last time I checked, Jesus left us here in it. Not only that, but we are to overcome it. If there is to be a wealth transfer from the fear and greed to those in The Kingdom, it will only come when we can walk in love. That means we are fair and fearless.

We find sensible, Godly instructions on how to do this in Galatians 5:13-26 and 6:7-9. Look at it from the New King James Version.

I say then; walk in the Spirit and you shall not fulfill the lust of the flesh. For the flesh lusts against the Spirit and Spirit against the flesh; and these are contrary to one another, so that you do not the things that you wish. But if you are led by the Spirit, you are not under the law.

Now the works of the flesh are evident, which are adultery, fornication, uncleanness, lewdness, idolatry, sorcery, hatred, contentions, jealousies, outbursts of wrath, selfish ambitions, and dissensions. heresies, envy, murders, drunkenness, revelries and the like; of which I tell you beforehand, just as I also told you in times past, that those who practice such things will not inherit the kingdom of God.

But the fruit of the Spirit is love, joy, peace. longsuffering, kindness, goodness, faithfulness, gentleness, self-control. Against such there is no law. And those who are Christ's have crucified the flesh with its passions and desires. If we live by the Spirit, let us also walk in the Spirit. Let us not become conceited, provoking one another, envying one another.

Do not be deceived, God is not mocked; for whatsoever a man sows, that he will also reap. For he who sows to his flesh will of the flesh reap corruption, but he who sows to the Spirit will of the Spirit reap everlasting life. And let us not grow weary while doing good, for in due season we shall reap if we do not lose heart. Therefore, as we have opportunity, let us do good to all, especially to those who are of the household of faith.

I believe there are four distinct areas in which we will never enjoy the freedom of walking in the Spirit unless we learn to walk in love. They are:

1. Fear of what any man can do to us.
2. Fear of Satan and what he can do to us.
3. Fear of the curse of the law, which are sickness, disease, poverty, mental disorders and death.

4. Fear of what God will or will not do. (Some fear He won't do what His Word says He'll do.)

Do you really know what the foundation of all fear is? Do you know that fear is what causes big egos, loud mouths, bad decisions, shady deals and a host of other ills that seem to so easily beset a Christian person in business?

That foundation of fear is one word: SELFISHNESS. What will people think, or what will happen to poor ole misunderstood me? If I don't get what I think I should, what will happen? If I do so and so and it makes me look foolish to those at the country club, what will that do to me? If I am not as successful as someone else, what does that mean? What if? What if? What if? The next worse questions we are prompted to ask are, "Why me? Why did that happen? Oh, I have the worst possible luck in life!"

Remember what happened to Job. He said, "Those things which I greatly feared have happened to me." He thought it, said it and got it.

The answer is in Romans 8:31. It says it best. *If God is for us, who can be against us?*

Jesus walked in this corrupt world and completed His mission. He never feared and was never selfish. Look at how He ended up. He sits at His Father's right hand, He is commander-in-chief of the angels of God, He is in charge of preparing the church for His return and He certainly wasn't a patsy. He fought when He had to and loved all the time.

All we have to do is work to be just like Him.